Diet recommendations for wholefood

Please check these recommendations always with a nutrition consultant, therapist, doctor or dietician. The recipes and the list of ingredients are supporting the conventional medical therapy.
The calorie disclosures of fresh ingredients (fruit and vegetables) vary according to quality and time of harvest. The contents were checked by a dietician and a nutrition consultant for the Traditional Chinese Medicine (TCM).

Author:
©2017 Josef Miligui
www.ebns.at

AF236888

Source:
The lists are created from the EBNS database for nutritional counseling. The database is used by dietitians, therapists and doctors for advising the patient / client.

Literature:
The specialist literature and the training documents of the German and Austrian dietary and traditional Chinese medicine serve as a knowledge base. We have used the documents as a basis of knowledge, adapted it to our experience and completed them.
http://di-book.com

Title Photo:
©2008 Erika Weixlbaumer

Production and publishing:
BoD – Books on Demand, Norderstedt
ISBN: 9783752811261

Diet recommendations for DIETETICS - Universal - Wholefood

1 Treatment strategy

Observe the WHO dietary recommendations / nutritional requirements rules (world health organization)
Tasty but mild seasoning and use herbs.
Corresponding preparation.
Take individual incompatibilities into account.
Food and drinks should not be too hot and not too cold.
Eat slowly and chew well so that the bite is poured and warmed up.
Light coffee, little or no alcohol and drinks with little or no sugar.
Make food fresh and low in fat.
Low-fat cooking techniques: steaming, cooking, steaming, cooking in foil and in the Roman pot.
Do not overheat the fats (no strong roast products).
Food must be cooked enough.

2 Avoid

Alcohol, smoking, very sharp, strongly spiced, heavy fat or sugary food.

3 Breakfast

kkal. per serving

Apple - banana cream.. 110
Apricot and cranberry ice cream.. 106
Banana Soymilk... 125
Barley and vegetable soup.. 281
Barley mash with steamed pear 113
Boiled celery salad with exotic spices.. 165
Breakfast - low protein... 575
Breakfast - Rice with fruits.. 230
Breakfast with cheese 593
Broccoli and Parmesan spread on toast bread 148
Carrot Risotto.. 308
Carrot soup... 209
Coffee.. 16
Colorful tuscan bean soup.. 249
Compote of local fruit and dried fruit... 45
Corn coffee with cardamom... 3
Cottage cheese with steamed fruit... 214
Couscous Salad... 338
Cream cheese substitute... 526
Curdcheesedumplings on strawberry pulp 553
Curry rice with raisins and nuts... 275
Fish soup with rosemary 271
Hearty polenta mash.. 262
Hearty winter breakfast 678
Hungarian rice salad 421
Lettuce with vinegar dressing 67
Mango banana yoghurt drink ice cold 121
Millet with pears 213
Noodles with vegetable and tomato sauce.................................. 561
Oat flakes with aromatic spices 280
Oyster mushrooms with asparagus 316
Plum Cake 502
Polenta with fried egg... 410
Polenta with peach... 197
Potato cream with herbs and fresh cheese 217
Rhubarb and apple jelly.. 180
Rhubarb cake with sprinkles.. 475

4 Snack

5 Lunch

6   Afternoon

7   Dinner

8   Any time

9 Recipes

(recommendable) = You can use more.
(little) = You should use less than specified or omit.

9.1 Andalusian fish pot

Strengthens immune system, prevents cancer, dissolves stagnation, promotes weight loss. Good to fight immunodeficiency, loss of appetite, flatulence, high blood pressure, depressions, diabetes, diarrhea, stimulates appetite.
Cooking time approx. 30 min
Calories p. portion: 348
4 portions
Allergens: ADLO

Quantity of ingredients
Basic recipe for a vegetable soup (nutritious) 2 cups / 500g. (yes)
Onion (spring onion) 2 pieces / 40g. (yes)
Olive oil 1 table spoon / 20g. (yes)
Lemon peel 1/2 piece / 3g. (yes)
Bay leaf 1 piece / 1g. (yes)
Potato 5/8 oz / 200g. (yes)
Cod 3/4 lbs / 300g. (recommended)
White wine 4 table spoons / 80g. (little)
Lemon juice 1/2 teaspoon / 10g. (yes)
Salt 1 pinch / 1g. (little)
Pepper (ground) 1 pinch / 0,2g. (yes)
Parsley 1 table spoon / 15g. (yes)
White bread (wheat bread) 8 slices / 250g. (little)

Cooking instructions:
Boil the vegetable broth with small spring onion, olive oil, grated lemon peel and bay leaf. Boil covered for 10 minutes. Add the peeled, diced potatoes and boil in about 8 minutes. Add fish pieces and white wine and switch to small heat. In the slightly boiling broth put the fish and boil it a few minutes. Season with lemon juice, salt and pepper. Serve with parsley sprinkled.
White bread as a side dish.

9.2   Apple - banana cream

Regulates gastrointestinal function, provides vitamin C, cholesterol lowering, reduces inflammation, diuretic, improves blood circulation.
Cooking time approx. 15 min
Calories p. portion: 110
4 portions
Allergens:

Quantity of ingredients
Apple (sour) 7/8 lbs / 400g. (recommended)
Water 3/4 cup - 6 oz / 200g. (yes)
Orange peel 1/4 piece / 5g. (yes)
Lemon peel 1/2 piece / 2g. (yes)
Sugar brown 2 teaspoons / 6g. (little)
Cinnamon sticks 1 piece / 0g. (yes)
Banana 1 piece / 150g. (yes)
Acerola fruit nectar or powder 1 teaspoon / 2g. (yes)
Orange juice 1/2 piece / 50g. (yes)
Lemon juice 1 table spoon / 10g. (yes)

Cooking instructions:
Cut the apple into fine slices, bring water to boil and add the apple slices, orange- and lemon peel, sugar and cinnamon and simmer about 7 minutes. The apples should be almost soft. Remove acerola and the cinnamon stick.
Mix the apple, the banana, the orange juice and the lemon juice.

9.3   Apricot and cranberry ice cream

Forces resistance to infections, good to fight oral mucosal inflammation, diarrhea. Has a positive effect on the urinary tract.
Cooking time approx. 5 min
Calories p. portion: 106
2 portions
Allergens:

Quantity of ingredients
Apricots 3/4 lbs / 350g. (yes)
Water 1/4 cup / 50g. (yes)
Cranberry 2 table spoons / 45g. (recommended)

Cooking instructions:
Mix the apricot juice with the cranberry syrup. Fill the juice into little molds, place in the freezer and let it freeze in about 3 hours.

9.4   Asparagus Cream Soup

Diuretic, improves blood circulation, prevents cancer, laxative, antiparasitic, stimulates liver function, good to fight loss of appetite, flatulence, rheumatism, heartburn.
Cooking time approx. 45 min
Calories p. portion: 240
2 portions
Allergens: ACG

Quantity of ingredients
Asparagus (green or white) 5/8 oz / 200g. (recommended)
Water 2 cup / 500g. (yes)
Rapeseed oil 2 table spoons / 30g. (recommended)
Wheat flour 2 table spoons / 10g. (yes)
Chicken yolk 1 piece / 25g. (little)
Cow's milk (whole milk 3.5% fat) 1 table spoon / 15g. (yes)
Sour cream 15% fat 1 table spoon / 15g. (yes)
Pepper (ground) 1 pinch / 0,5g. (yes)
Nutmeg 1 pinch / 0,5g. (yes)
Lemon juice 1 teaspoon / 2g. (yes)
Parsley 2 table spoons / 20g. (yes)
Salt 1 pinch / 1g. (little)

Cooking instructions:
Wash and peel the asparagus.
Heat water, a little lemon juice and pinch of salt till it boils. Tie the asparagus spears together.
Add the asparagus peel to the cooking water and bring to the boil.
Add the asparagus and cook on low heat for about 20 minutes.
Then remove the asparagus bunches and pour the broth through a sieve.
For the roux, heat the oil in a saucepan, add the flour and sauté until it is colorless, slowly top up with the asparagus sauce and simmer for 10 minutes.
Cut the asparagus spears into pieces about 3 cm long and place them to the soup.

Just before serving, bring the soup to the boil again.
Mix the egg yolk with the milk and sour cream.
Remove the pot from the heat and stir in the egg yolk and milk mixture.
Season with pepper and nutmeg, decorate with the chopped parsley
and serve immediately.

9.5 Banana Soymilk

Good to fight loss of appetite, oral mucosa inflammation. Strengthens
body energy, promotes stomach-spleen harmony, promotes digestion,
regulates gastrointestinal function. Relieves pain, detoxifying,
bactericide.
Cooking time approx. 5 min
Calories p. portion: 126
2 portions
Allergens: E

Quantity of ingredients
Banana 1 piece / 120g. (yes)
Soybean milk 1 1/2 cups / 400g. (yes)
Honey 1 teaspoon / 3g. (yes)
Cinnamon ground 1 pinch / 1g. (yes)
Acerola fruit nectar or powder 1 teaspoon / 2g. (yes)

Cooking instructions:
Cut the banana into pieces, puree them with soy milk, acerola, honey
and cinnamon with the mixing stick.

9.6 Barley and vegetable soup

Supports urination, detoxifying, promotes spleen and liver, reduces
blood pressure, strengthens immune system, prevents cancer, reduces
radiation damage, promotes digestion, helps to digest fat, harmonizes
metabolism.
Cooking time approx. 2 hours
Calories p. portion: 281
3 portions
Allergens: AGL

Quantity of ingredients
Barley 1 cup / 120g. (yes)
Shiitake, dried 1/8 oz / 4g. (yes)
Onion (shallot) 1 piece / 20g. (yes)
Cumin (Caraway seed) 1 knife tip / 0,5g. (yes)
Sunflower oil 1 table spoon / 10g. (yes)
Water 1 cup / 250g. (yes)
Celery sticks 2 branches / 20g. (recommended)
Peas, green 5/8 lbs - 8oz / 250g. (yes)
Tomato 1 piece / 50g. (recommended)
Carrot 2 pieces / 150g. (recommended)
French beans Handful / 30g. (yes)
Salt 1 pinch / 1g. (little)
Pepper (ground) 1 pinch / 0,5g. (yes)
Parsley 1 teaspoon / 3g. (yes)
Butter organic 1 teaspoon / 3g. (yes)

Cooking instructions:
Soak the barley in the evening for the next day. Soak the mushrooms separately at the next day. Brown onion and cumin in oil, then boil with water. Add the chopped vegetables, some salt, the barley and the shiitake mushrooms and cook everything to a thick soup. At the end, season with pepper, parsley and a little butter.

9.7 Barley mash with steamed pear

Promotes digestion, supports urination, promotes spleen, diuretic, forcing spleen, relaxes, promotes perspiration.
Cooking time approx. 25 min
Calories p. portion: 114
5 portions
Allergens: A

Quantity of ingredients
Water 10 cups / 1200g. (yes)
Barley 1 cup / 120g. (yes)
Ginger fresh 2 slices / 2g. (yes)
Cardamom 3 capsules / 1g. (yes)
Salt 1 pinch / 1g. (little)
Pear 1 piece / 200g. (recommended)
Sugar cane sugar 1/2 teaspoon / 5g. (little)

Cooking instructions:
Grind coarse the barley and roast it dry. Add hot water, add ginger and cardamom and let it swell to a pulp in low heat. Peel and dice the pear and boil for 10 minutes with a little water. At the end, add the stewed pear, a little butter and sweetener.

Variant: If you want to go fast, you can use barley flakes instead of shot.

9.8   Basic recipe for a beef broth (clear)

Strengthens muscles, tendons and bones, reduces blood pressure, strengthens immune system, prevents cancer, reduces radiation damage, stimulates digestion, reduces pain, promotes digestion, diuretic. Rosemary stimulates digestion.
Cooking time approx. 4-8 hours
Calories p. portion: 114
10 portions
Allergens: O

Quantity of ingredients
Beef soup meat 1,1 lbs / 500g. (yes)
Beef meatbones 5/8 oz / 200g. (yes)
Vinegar (Red wine vinegar) 1 dash / 3g. (yes)
Juniper berry 8 pieces / 6g. (recommended)
Rosemary 1 pinch / 1g. (yes)
Carrot 3 pieces / 210g. (recommended)
Parsnip 2 pieces / 300g. (yes)
Leek 1 piece / 200g. (yes)
Ginger fresh 1/2 teaspoon / 5g. (yes)
Lovage 1 stem / 15g. (yes)
Clove 2 pieces / 2g. (yes)
Pimento 6 pieces / 12g. (yes)
Anise (Common Fennel) 2 pieces / 1g. (yes)
Salt 1 teaspoon / 5g. (little)
Water 3,3 lbs / 1300g. (yes)

Cooking instructions:
Heat water, a dash of red wine vinegar, some juniper berries, a little rosemary, bones and meat till it boils; add carrot, parsnip, leek, ginger, lovage, clove, allspice, star anise and a little salt; simmer for 4-8 hours then strain.
Refrigerate for later use.

9.9 Basic recipe for a chicken broth worming

Strengthens blood, strengthens bone marrow, reduces blood pressure, strengthens immune system, prevents cancer, reduces radiation damage, promotes sweating, dissolves stagnation, good to fight loss of appetite, flatulence.
Cooking time approx. 2-3 hours
Calories p. portion: 90
9 portions
Allergens: L

Quantity of ingredients
Chicken meat 1/2 piece / 600g. (yes)
Carrot 2 pieces / 150g. (recommended)
Leek 1 stick / 45g. (yes)
Celery root 1 piece / 500g. (recommended)
Ginger fresh 2 slices / 2g. (yes)
Fenugreek (Trigonella foenum-graecum) 1 teaspoon / 2g. (yes)
Juniper berry 1 teaspoon / 3g. (recommended)
Bay leaf 3 pieces / 2g. (yes)
Water 4 cup / 900g. (yes)

Cooking instructions:
Remove chicken parts from fat. Place chicken pieces in a saucepan with hot water and heat till it boils briefly, skimming any resulting foam. Add coarsely chopped vegetables and all spices and cook over medium heat for 2 to 3 hours. Strain the finished soup. Throw away vegetables and bones.
Tip: If you want to use the meat as a soup insert, take out after 45 minutes and return only the bones in the soup.
Refrigerate for later use.

9.10 Basic recipe for a duck broth

Forcing spleen, strengthens blood, supports urination, reduces blood pressure, strengthens immune system, prevents cancer, reduces radiation damage.
Cooking time approx. 2-3 hours
Calories p. portion: 61
6 portions
Allergens: L

Quantity of ingredients
Water 2 cup / 450g. (yes)
Duck (heart) 5/8 oz / 200g. (yes)
Duck (slaughtered) 1/4 lbs - 4oz / 100g. (yes)
Carrot 2 pieces / 100g. (recommended)
Celery root 1/2 piece / 600g. (recommended)

Cooking instructions:
Cook duck pieces with vegetables for 2-3 hours. Sift broth through a
fine sieve and refrigerate for later use.
The innards can be reused: You cut them finely and leaves them for a
few minutes with fresh vegetables in the broth draw. Sprinkle with
parsley before serving.

9.11 Basic recipe for a fish broth

Strengthens the kidneys, promotes watering, reduces blood pressure,
strengthens immune system, prevents cancer, reduces radiation
damage. Low in cholesterol and protein rich. Improves blood circulation,
stimulates appetite.
Cooking time approx. 40 min
Calories p. portion: 128
5 portions
Allergens: DLO

Quantity of ingredients
Fish pieces mixed (fresh water) 3/4 lbs / 300g. (recommended)
Celery root 1/4 lbs - 4oz / 120g. (recommended)
Leek 2 inches / 10g. (yes)
Carrot 2 pieces / 150g. (recommended)
White wine 1/2 cup / 125g. (little)
Lemon 1/2 piece / 50g. (yes)
Bay leaf 2 leaves / 2g. (yes)
Peppercorns 3 pieces / 2g. (yes)
Olive oil 1 table spoon / 10g. (yes)
Water 2 cup / 450g. (yes)

Cooking instructions:
Fry celery, chopped carrots and leeks in olive oil, add bay leaf and
peppercorns, add pieces of fish and sauté briefly. Add water, add little
white wine or lemon. Simmer gently for 30 minutes. Skim off the
resulting foam several times. In the end, sift the ingredients through a
cloth. Refrigerate for later use

9.12 Basic recipe for a reissue soup (Congee)

Low fat content, for the drainage of the body overweight and high blood pressure.
Cooking time approx. 2-4 hours
Calories p. portion: 140
3 portions
Allergens:

Quantity of ingredients
Rice variety any 1 cup / 120g. (yes)
Water 6 cups / 700g. (yes)

Cooking instructions:
Cook rice and water in a ratio of about 1: 6. The amount of water determines the thickness of the mash (matter of taste).
Put the rice in a saucepan with a heavy lid. It is important to simmer the rice after a short boil on the slightest flame, otherwise it burns.
Boil the rice for 2-4 hours. The longer he cooks, the more he strengthens.
If you want to eat the dish for breakfast, you can put the rice on just before bedtime.
To be on the safe side, you should first check the behavior of your pot and cooker under observation for a similar amount of time, so that nothing burns.
Refrigerate for later use.

9.13 Basic recipe for a vegetable soup, nutritious

Reduces blood pressure, strengthens immune system, prevents cancer, forcing spleen, dissolves stagnation, promotes weight loss. Good to fight immunodeficiency, high blood pressure, depressions, diabetes, diarrhea, reduces blood lipids.
Cooking time approx. 2-3 hours
Calories p. portion: 48
5 portions
Allergens: L

Quantity of ingredients
Olive oil 1 table spoon / 4g. (yes)
Onion white 1 piece / 60g. (yes)
Carrot 3 pieces / 200g. (recommended)
Parsnip 3/8 lbs - 6oz / 150g. (yes)
Celery root 1 cup / 100g. (recommended)

Ginger fresh 1/2 teaspoon / 2g. (yes)
Lemon 1/2 piece / 25g. (yes)
Juniper berry 6 pieces / 6g. (recommended)
Thyme dried 1 pinch / 1g. (yes)
Lovage 1 table spoon / 3g. (yes)
Bay leaf 2 leaves / 1g. (yes)
Salt 1 pinch / 1g. (little)
Water 3 cups / 650g. (yes)

Cooking instructions:
Cut the vegetables into cubes.
Heat oil in hot pot, fry shortly onions and vegetables.
Add cold water, then add ginger, bay leaf and lemon juice.
Season with juniper, thyme and lovage. Cover for 2 - 3 hours on a low heat and simmer.
The used vegetables should be thrown away.
The basic recipe serves as a soup base and to refine vegetables, legumes or cereals.
If you want to eat vegetable soup immediately, add the desired vegetables half an hour before.
Refrigerate for later use.

9.14 Beef pumpkin and vegetable stew

Reduces inflammation, improves digestion, reduces blood glucose, strengthens the muscles, tendons and bones, promotes digestion, helps to digest fat.
Cooking time approx. 1 hour
Calories p. portion: 369
4 portions
Allergens: AL

Quantity of ingredients
Beef meat 3/4 lbs / 350g. (yes)
Pumpkin 3/4 lbs / 350g. (yes)
Leek 3/8 lbs - 6oz / 150g. (yes)
Potato 3/4 lbs / 350g. (yes)
Tomato 3/8 lbs - 6oz / 150g. (recommended)
Olive oil 2 table spoons / 25g. (yes)
Basic recipe for a vegetable soup (nutritious) 1/4 lbs - 4oz / 125g. (yes)
Salt 1 pinch / 1g. (little)
Pepper (ground) 1 pinch / 0,5g. (yes)

Peppers powder 1 teaspoon / 2g. (yes)
Ground caraway 1 pinch / 1g. (yes)
Sugar cane sugar 1 pinch / 1g. (little)
Parsley 1/2 bunch / 30g. (yes)
White bread (wheat bread) 4 slices / 80g. (little)

Cooking instructions:
Dice beef. Peel pumpkin and dice. Cut the leek into rings and dice the peeled potatoes.
Brew the tomatoes with boiling water, peel off the skin and dice.
Steam the meat in olive oil and fill with vegetable stock. Add the cleaned vegetables. Season with salt, pepper, paprika, cumin and fructose.
Stew for 30 minutes over low heat.
Season again and sprinkle with parsley and serve with white bread.

9.15 Beluga lentil stew with vegetables

Promotes sweating, dissolves stagnation. Relieves constipation, strengthens mother milk production, stimulates nerves, detoxifying, reduces inflammation, improves blood circulation. Strengthens heart and kidney, diuretic, calms the stomach, promotes digestion.
Cooking time approx. 20 min
Calories p. portion: 201
5 portions
Allergens:

Quantity of ingredients
Lentils 1 1/2 cups / 240g. (recommended)
Water 4-5 cups / 500g. (yes)
Carrot 3 pieces / 150g. (recommended)
Leek 1 piece / 300g. (yes)
Kohlrabi 1/2 piece / 200g. (recommended)
Tomato 2 pieces / 80g. (recommended)
Onion white 1 piece / 50g. (yes)
Bay leaf 2 leaves / 1g. (yes)
Fennel 1 piece / 250g. (recommended)
Star anise 2 pieces / 1g. (yes)
Juniper berry 6 pieces / 2g. (recommended)
Olive oil 2 table spoons / 30g. (yes)
Salt 1 pinch / 1g. (little)
Ginger fresh 1/2 teaspoon / 2g. (yes)
Black caraway 1 pinch / 1g. (yes)

Cooking instructions:
Heat oil in hot pot. Fry onions and add diced vegetables and spices, lentils (washed well) and salt. Cover with cold water (3 fingers wide) and cook for 20 minutes on a low heat.
Sprinkle with fresh herbs and black cumin

Goes well with rice!

9.16 Black root with yogurt

Stimulates kidney, bladder and forces the cleaning of the body. In the physiological sense, they generally stimulate the glands in the organism. Good to fight acute or chronic constipation of the intestine. Rich in Vitamins and trace elements.
Cooking time approx. 20 min
Calories p. portion: 424
2 portions
Allergens: AG

Quantity of ingredients
Salsify 1 lbs / 400g. (yes)
Yogurt (natural, 1.5% fat) 4 table spoons / 80g. (recommended)
Herbs various 1 table spoon / 8g. (yes)
Salt 1 pinch / 1g. (little)
Herbs various 2 table spoons / 6g. (yes)
Multi-grain bread (gray bread) 6 slices / 120g. (yes)

Cooking instructions:
Peel the salsify and simmer in salted water until tender. Pour away the water, cool the salsify and cut it to size.
Cover with yoghurt and sprinkle with fresh herbs. Serve with the bread. You can also use the salsify from the conserve.

9.17 Boiled celery salad with exotic spices

Forcing spleen, relieves diarrhea, antibacterial, blood-forming, blood detoxifying, reduces inflammation, diuretic, improves blood circulation.
Cooking time approx. 30 min
Calories p. portion: 166
4 portions
Allergens: GLMNO

Quantity of ingredients
Celery root 1 1/2 piece / 900g. (recommended)
Yogurt (natural, 3.5% fat) 1 cup / 250g. (yes)
Sour cream 15% fat 2 table spoons / 20g. (yes)
Turmeric (yellow root) 1 pinch / 1g. (yes)
Sesame oil 1 table spoon / 20g. (recommended)
Pepper (ground) 1 pinch / 0,5g. (yes)
Lemongrass 1 pinch / 1g. (yes)
Onion white 1/2 piece / 25g. (yes)
Mustard 1/2 teaspoon / 1g. (yes)
Black caraway 1 pinch / 1g. (yes)
Salt 1 pinch / 1g. (little)
Lemon juice 1 piece / 40g. (yes)
Apple (sour) 1/2 piece / 100g. (recommended)
Peppers powder 1 pinch / 1g. (yes)
Vinegar (Apple vinegar) 1 dash / 3g. (yes)

Cooking instructions:
Cook the peeled celeriac in thick slices and then cut into bite-sized strips.

Dressing: Mix a little yoghurt, sour cream, turmeric, sesame oil, pepper, lemongrass powder, finely chopped onion, a little mustard, salt, crushed black cumin, some cold water, lemon juice or vinegar; add the sour chopped apple, some rose paprika, the lukewarm celery and mix well; let it rest for 2 - 3 hours or overnight.

Ideal as a substitute for raw food

9.18 Breakfast - low protein

Increase appetite, detoxifying, increases blood glucose levels, harmonizes heart rhythm, good to fight vomiting, nutritional disorders, diarrhea.
Cooking time approx. 10 min
Calories p. portion: 575
1 portions
Allergens: GO

Quantity of ingredients
Bread with carob kernel flour 3 oz / 80g. (yes)
Butter organic 1/2 oz / 20g. (yes)
Apricot jam 1 oz / 30g. (yes)
Fresh cheese with herbs 1 oz / 30g. (yes)
Coffee 1/2 cup / 150g. (yes)
Sugar white 1/2 oz / 10g. (little)

Cooking instructions:
Prepare coffee to taste, make fresh cheese if possible with fresh herbs
yourself.

9.19 Breakfast - Rice with fruits

Good to fight blood circulation disorders, thrombose, risk of embolism,
high blood pressure, a headache, heart attack and stroke. Encourages
blood build-up, promotes digestion, reduces Inflammation.
Cooking time approx. 10 min - 3 hours
Calories p. portion: 231
3 portions
Allergens: GHO

Quantity of ingredients
Basic recipe for a rice soup (Congee) 6 cups / 500g. (yes)
Cow's milk (whole milk 3.5% fat) 1/2 to 1 cup / 80g. (yes)
Honey 1 table spoon / 10g. (yes)
Butter organic 1 table spoon / 15g. (yes)
Dates dried 1 table spoon / 15g. (yes)
Fig 1 table spoon / 15g. (yes)
Apple (sour) 1 piece / 200g. (recommended)
Hazelnuts 1/2 teaspoon / 5g. (yes)
Almond 1/2 teaspoon / 5g. (yes)
Cinnamon ground 1 pinch / 1g. (yes)

Cooking instructions:
Cook rice congee according to basic recipe or use pre-cooked.
Make it with the milk more fluid and sweet with honey.
Fry the fruits and nuts in butter and mix with the finished rice soup, add
chopped dates, figs and the apple.

9.20 Breakfast with cheese

Good to fight weakness, stomach pressure, belching, diabetes, acute or chronic obstruction of the bowel, skin problems. Coffee supports urinating, stimulates appetite, detoxifying, increases blood glucose levels, harmonizes heart rhythm.
Cooking time approx. 10 min
Calories p. portion: 593
1 portions
Allergens: AGO

Quantity of ingredients
Water 1 cup / 120g. (yes)
Coffee 2 teaspoons / 4g. (yes)
Whole grain bread 2 slices / 100g. (recommended)
Margarine 1/2 oz / 10g. (yes)
Edam cheese 1 oz / 30g. (yes)
Strawberry jam 1/2 oz / 20g. (yes)
Curd cheese 20% 1/8 lbs - 2oz / 40g. (recommended)

Cooking instructions:
Prepare coffee as usual. Avoid sugar or use sweetener. Cover the bread slices with margarine and put the cheese and marmalade on the breakfast table. Decorating decoratively increases your appetite.

9.21 Broccoli and Parmesan spread on toast bread

Good to fight loss of appetite, blood clotting, thyroid function, increase Vitamin B12, strengthen immune system, good to fight belching, diabetes, acute or chronic constipation, dissolves stagnation.
Cooking time approx. 15 min
Calories p. portion: 148
2 portions
Allergens: AG

Quantity of ingredients
Broccoli 5/8 oz / 200g. (recommended)
Curd cheese 20% 3 oz / 80g. (recommended)
Yogurt (natural, 1.5% fat) 1 table spoon / 10g. (recommended)
Parmesan 2 table spoons / 15g. (yes)
Lemon peel 1/2 teaspoon / 1g. (yes)
Basil (fresh) 1 table spoon / 5g. (yes)
Chives 1 table spoon / 5g. (yes)
Salt 1 pinch / 1g. (little)

Pepper (ground) 1 pinch / 0,3g. (yes)
Toast bread (whole grain) 6 slices / 24g. (yes)

Cooking instructions:
Cook broccoli in a sieve insert over steam for 8 minutes until firm. Finely chop broccoli.
Mix the curd, yoghurt, parmesan and lemon peel well. Mix cheese cream with broccoli, basil and chives. Season the spread with salt and pepper. Serve on the crunchy toasted toast.

9.22 Broccoli cream soup

Strengthen your immune system, build and maintain healthy bones, teeth, hair and nails. Reduces blood pressure, strengthens immune system, prevents cancer, reduces radiation damage.
Cooking time approx. 30 min
Calories p. portion: 98
6 portions
Allergens: LO

Quantity of ingredients
Olive oil 2 table spoons / 7g. (yes)
Broccoli 1,1 lbs / 500g. (recommended)
Carrot 2 pieces / 150g. (recommended)
Potato 2 pieces / 120g. (yes)
Onion white 1 piece / 50g. (yes)
Water 1 cup / 50g. (yes)
Basic recipe for a vegetable soup (nutritious) 2 cup / 500g. (yes)
White wine 1/2 cup / 125g. (little)
Sage 1 teaspoon / 2g. (yes)
Rosemary 1 teaspoon / 2g. (yes)
Pepper (ground) 1 pinch / 0,5g. (yes)
Salt 1 pinch / 1g. (little)

Cooking instructions:
Add the olive oil to the pan, add the washed and cut broccoli, diced carrots and potatoes, sauté for a short time, add the chopped onion, fill with water, enough water to cover the vegetables at least 3 finger breadths. Add bouillon, salt, add a little bit of white wine, add the seasoned sage and rosemary.
Heat till it boils and then simmer on a small fire for about 25 minutes. Season with pepper, if necessary season with sea salt. Purée the soup.

9.23 Carrot and millet bake with apple compote

Promotes spleen and liver, reduces blood pressure, strengthens immune system, prevents cancer, calms nerves and stomach, diuretic, good to fight chronic constipation of the intestine.
Cooking time approx. 1 hour
Calories p. portion: 350
7 portions
Allergens: CGH

Quantity of ingredients
Millet 5/8 oz / 200g. (yes)
Cow's milk (whole milk 3.5% fat) 2 cups / 450g. (yes)
Lemon peel 1/2 piece / 2g. (yes)
Sugar brown 2 table spoons / 20g. (little)
Carrot 7/8 lbs / 400g. (recommended)
Ginger fresh 2 teaspoons / 6g. (yes)
Acerola fruit nectar or powder 1 teaspoon / 2g. (yes)
Almond puree 1/8 lbs - 2oz / 50g. (yes)
Chicken egg 4 pieces / 240g. (yes)
Yogurt (natural, 1.5% fat) 3/8 lbs - 6oz / 150g. (recommended)
Butter organic 1 teaspoon / 4g. (yes)
Apple (sour) 4 pieces / 600g. (recommended)
Water 1 cup / 300g. (yes)
Clove 2 pieces / 1g. (yes)
Sugar brown 1 table spoon / 10g. (little)

Cooking instructions:
Preheat the oven to 100°C/212°F (with circulating air 8o°C/176°F, gas level 2).
Heat the milk with the millet till it boils, add lemon zest and sugar. Cover and simmer for 5 minutes, then simmer in a preheated oven for 20 minutes. Switch oven to medium heat.
Peel apples and cut into small pieces, boil with water, cloves and sugar for about 5 minutes.
Mix the millet in a bowl with the grated carrots, finely chopped ginger and acerola.
Mix the almond paste (or butter) with the hand mixer. Add egg yolk and stir everything to a smooth cream. Mix in sour cream. Add millet and carrots.
Beat the egg whites very stiff and lift them under the millet pulp. Brush out a baking dish with butter. Add the millet and bake in a preheated oven for 45 minutes on a low heat. Serve with the apple compote.

9.24 Carrot Risotto

Strengthens immune system, prevents cancer, loss of appetite, flatulence, high blood pressure, depressions, diabetes, diarrhea, stimulates liver function, dissolves stagnation.
Cooking time approx. 45 min
Calories p. portion: 308
2 portions
Allergens: GL

Quantity of ingredients
Olive oil 1/2 teaspoon / 5g. (yes)
Onion (spring onion) 2 table spoons / 7g. (yes)
Nutmeg 1 pinch / 0,3g. (yes)
Parsley 1/2 bunch / 25g. (yes)
Rice variety any 1/4 lbs - 4oz / 100g. (yes)
Carrot 5/8 lbs - 8oz / 250g. (recommended)
Basic recipe for a vegetable soup (nutritious) 1 cup / 280g. (yes)
Fennel seeds ground 1/4 teaspoon / 1g. (yes)
Basil (fresh) 1/2 teaspoon / 2g. (yes)
Salt 1 pinch / 1g. (little)
Pepper (ground) 1 pinch / 0,3g. (yes)
Parmesan 1 table spoon / 10g. (yes)

Cooking instructions:
Heat the oil in a pan, fry the onions in a glassy and very soft manner. Add parsley, sauté briefly. Add rice, carrots and nutmeg, sauté briefly while stirring. Add the vegetable stock, season with fennel and basil, heat till it boils and cook for about 20 minutes until the rice and carrots are well. Stir from time to time and add some vegetable stock if necessary. The risotto should be slightly soupy. Just before the end of the cooking time mix in the white wine and simmer the risotto for a short while. Remove risotto from the heat, mix in Parmesan.

9.25 Carrot soup

Promotes spleen and liver, reduces blood pressure, strengthens immune system, prevents cancer, reduces radiation damage, improves blood circulation, improves medication effect, increase Appetite, stimulates liver function.
Cooking time approx. 30 min
Calories p. portion: 210
2 portions
Allergens: O

Quantity of ingredients
Carrot 1,1 lbs / 500g. (recommended)
Pepper (ground) 1 pinch / 0,5g. (yes)
Nutmeg 1 pinch / 1g. (yes)
Salt 1 pinch / 1g. (little)
White wine 1/2 cup / 125g. (little)
Orange juice Alternatively for wine / g. (yes)
Parsley 2 table spoons / 10g. (yes)
Peppers powder 1 pinch / 1g. (yes)
Thyme dried Alternative to rose paprika / g. (yes)
Pine nuts 1 table spoon / 15g. (yes)
Sunflower seeds Alternatively to pine nuts / g. (yes)

Cooking instructions:
Place peeled large cut carrot pieces in hot water; cook and then puree;
season with ground pepper, a little nutmeg, a pinch of salt; add a dash
of white wine and simmer for a few minutes or season with orange
juice; Add parsley as desired; stir in some rose paprika or fresh thyme;
sprinkle with roasted pine nuts or sunflower seeds before serving.

9.26 Celery and potato cream soup

Reduces blood pressure, strengthens immune system, promotes weight
loss. Good to fight immunodeficiency, loss of appetite, flatulence,
depressions, diabetes, diarrhea, improves digestion.
Cooking time approx. 45 min
Calories p. portion: 113
4 portions
Allergens: GL

Quantity of ingredients
Olive oil 1 table spoon / 10g. (yes)
Onion white 1/2 piece / 25g. (yes)
Basic recipe for a vegetable soup (nutritious) 3 cups / 700g. (yes)
Potato 5/8 oz / 200g. (yes)
Nutmeg 1 pinch / 0,5g. (yes)
Ground 1 pinch / 0,5g. (yes)
Lemon peel 1/4 piece / 1g. (yes)
Créme fraiche cheese 2 table spoons / 20g. (yes)
Salt 1 pinch / 1g. (little)
Parsley 1 table spoon / 8g. (yes)

Cooking instructions:
Heat the olive oil in a saucepan lightly. Fry the onions very gently in a mild heat. Pour with vegetable stock according to the basic recipe. Cover and cook for 15 minutes.
Add curd-cut potato, celery, nutmeg, cumin and lemon zest. Spice with salt and cook for 12 minutes. Potatoes and celery should be soft. Remove the lemon peel.
Puree the soup with crème fraiche using a blender. Season the soup with salt.
Arrange the soup in portions with the chopped parsley.

9.27 Champignon salad with cress

Promotes digestion and is good to fight high blood pressure. Good to fight loss of appetite, improves blood circulation.
Cooking time approx. 5 min
Calories p. portion: 220
1 portions
Allergens: AN

Quantity of ingredients
Champignon 5/8 lbs - 8oz / 250g. (yes)
Sesame oil 2 table spoons / 6g. (recommended)
Pepper (ground) 1 pinch / 0,5g. (yes)
Salt 1 pinch / 1g. (little)
Lemon 1/2 piece / 15g. (yes)
Peppers powder 2 pinches / 0,1g. (yes)
Cress 2 table spoons / 10g. (yes)
White bread (wheat bread) 2 slices / 30g. (little)

Cooking instructions:
Cut mushrooms into thin slices.
Dressing: sesame oil, a little ground pepper, salt, plenty of lemon juice, stir well the rose pepper; give over the finely chopped mushrooms; plenty of watercress.
Goes well with: white bread, round grain rice or quinoa; Along with the cereal, the salad makes a simple, light meal.
Serve with white bread.

9.28 Chicory salad with tangerine

Dissolves mucus, is rich in A-B-C Vitamins, promotes digestion, forcing spleen, promotes weight loss. Good to fight loss of appetite, flatulence, immunodeficiency.
Cooking time approx. 10 min
Calories p. portion: 257
3 portions
Allergens: AGNO

Quantity of ingredients
Tangerine 4 pieces / 300g. (yes)
Chicory 2-3 pieces / 300g. (recommended)
Sesame oil 2 table spoons / 18g. (recommended)
Pepper (ground) 1 pinch / 0,5g. (yes)
Salt 1 pinch / 1g. (little)
Vinegar Aceto Balsamico 2 teaspoons / 6g. (yes)
Orange 1/2 piece / 70g. (yes)
Lemon 1/2 piece / 25g. (yes)
Peppers powder 1 pinch / 1g. (yes)
Orange jam 1 teaspoon / 4g. (yes)
Cream, sweet 30% 1 table spoon / 10g. (little)
White bread (wheat bread) 6 slices / 120g. (little)

Cooking instructions:
Peel tangerines and cut into bite-sized pieces; Cut chicory roughly and mix well.
Dressing: sesame oil, pepper, salt, raspberry vinegar or balsamic vinegar, a little lemon or orange juice, rose paprika, orange marmalade or, alternatively, another jam, stir well. Give a little sweet cream over the salad and let it pass briefly.

9.29 Coffee

Supports urination, stimulates appetite, detoxifying, increases blood glucose levels, harmonizes heart rhythm.
Cooking time approx. 5 min
Calories p. portion: 16
1 portions
Allergens:

Quantity of ingredients
Coffee 1 table spoon / 5g. (yes)
Water 1 cup / 120g. (yes)
Sugar white 1 teaspoon / 4g. (little)

Cooking instructions:
Depending on your taste, prepare a filter coffee, espresso or "Turkish".

9.30 Cold cherry soup with curd cheese dumpling

Improves blood circulation, reduces inflammation, good to fight
weakness, belching, diabetes, acute or chronic obstruction of the bowel.
Laxative, stimulates digestion, cleans the intestinal flora.
Cooking time approx. 2 hours and more
Calories p. portion: 320
2 portions
Allergens: GO

Quantity of ingredients
Cherry compote 7/8 lbs / 450g. (yes)
Agar agar (kelp) 1/2 teaspoon / 1,5g. (yes)
Curd cheese 20% 1/4 lbs - 4oz / 100g. (recommended)
Sour cream 15% fat 1/8 lbs - 2oz / 50g. (yes)
Vanilla sugar natural 1 package / 1g. (yes)
Sugar brown 1 table spoon / 10g. (little)
Cinnamon ground 1 pinch / 0,5g. (yes)
Lemon peel 1 pinch / 1g. (yes)

Cooking instructions:
Strain the cherry compote.
Finely puree half of the cherries with the cherry juice using a blender
and pass through a sieve.
Stir agar agar powder with cold water until smooth.
Bring the cherry puree to boil while stirring.
Mix in the agar-agar and cook the cherry puree for 1 minute while
stirring.
Spread hot cherry puree on two soup plates.
Sprinkle the remaining cherries into the soup.
Cool down cherry soup for 2 hours until lightly gelled.
Use the hand mixer to stir the cord cheese, sour cream, sugar, vanilla
sugar, cinnamon and lemon zest into a smooth, firm cream.
From the cream with the tablespoon, prick small dumplings and put
them into the cherry soup.

9.31 Colorful Tuscan bean soup

Promotes digestion, helps to digest fat, supports urination, reduces blood pressure, diuretic, calms the stomach.
Cooking time approx. 2 hours
Calories p. portion: 249
3 portions
Allergens: L

Quantity of ingredients
Kidney beans (red) 1/8 lbs - 2oz / 50g. (yes)
Chickpeas 1 oz / 25g. (yes)
Lentils 1 oz / 25g. (recommended)
Celery sticks 1 stick / 10g. (recommended)
Tomato 2 pieces / 100g. (recommended)
Fennel seeds ground 1/2 teaspoon / 1g. (yes)
Salt 1 pinch / 1g. (little)
Pepper (ground) 1 pinch / 0,5g. (yes)
Garlic 1 clove / 3g. (yes)
Olive oil 2 table spoons / 50g. (yes)
Water 2 1/4 cups / 500g. (yes)
Basil (fresh) 5-7 leaves / 3g. (yes)

Cooking instructions:
Soak legumes, boil and puree. Add vegetables, spices, herbs and oil and cook gently for 2 hours.
Variation: Sweet chestnuts give the dish a special Italian touch.

9.32 Compote of local fruit and dried fruit

Promotes digestion, supports urination, stops diarrhea, promotes digestion, appetizing, relieves diarrhea. Warms stomach and spleen, improves blood circulation.
Cooking time approx. 15 min
Calories p. portion: 45
4 portions
Allergens:

Quantity of ingredients
Apple (sweet) 1 piece / 150g. (recommended)
Pear 1 piece / 150g. (recommended)
Cinnamon ground 1 pinch / 0,2g. (yes)
Lemon peel 1/2 teaspoon / 2g. (yes)
Water 2 cup / 500g. (yes)

Cooking instructions:
Cook the apple and pear with the dried fruit until soft. Sprinkle with cinnamon and lemon zest (organic).

9.33 Corn coffee with cardamom

Diuretic, forcing spleen, supports urination, relaxes, reduces fat.
Cooking time approx. 5 min
Calories p. portion: 3
1 portions
Allergens:

Quantity of ingredients
Cereal coffee 1 table spoon / 15g. (yes)
Cardamom 2 cores / 1g. (yes)
Water 1 cup / 120g. (yes)

Cooking instructions:
Boil water, coffee, sugar and cardamom. Let it set for one min before drinking.

9.34 Cottage cheese with steamed fruit

Good to fight loss of appetite, promotes digestion, supports urination.
Cooking time approx. 20 min
Calories p. portion: 214
2 portions
Allergens: G

Quantity of ingredients
Cottage cheese 3/4 lbs / 300g. (yes)
Apple (sour) 1 piece / 100g. (recommended)
Pear 1 piece / 100g. (recommended)

Cooking instructions:
Wash apples and pears well, do not peel, and chop small. In a pot with steam filter, boil them al dente, remove and allow to cool down.
Serve the cheese, spread the fruit on it.

9.35 Couscous Salad

Forcing spleen, promotes digestion, stimulates liver function, reduces blood pressure, strengthens immune system, diuretic.
Cooking time approx. 25 min
Calories p. portion: 338
3 portions
Allergens: A

Quantity of ingredients
Water 1 cup / 100g. (yes)
Olive oil 1 table spoon / 15g. (yes)
Couscous 5/8 oz / 200g. (yes)
Lemon juice 2 table spoons / 30g. (yes)
Lemon peel 1 teaspoon / 2g. (yes)
Tomato 2 pieces / 80g. (recommended)
Cucumber 1/4 lbs - 4oz / 100g. (recommended)
Carrot 1/4 lbs - 4oz / 100g. (recommended)
Parsley 1 Bunch / 100g. (yes)
Chives 1 Bunch / 100g. (yes)
Peppermint 3 twigs / 30g. (yes)

Cooking instructions:
Boil in a small saucepan 250 ml. water with salt and 1 tablespoon olive oil. Add the couscous, take the stove in the front and let it swell covered for 5 minutes. Put the couscous back on the stove and let it simmer for about 2 minutes with gentle stirring. If necessary, add 1 - 3 tbsp of hot water.
Mix the couscous with lemon juice, chopped lemon peel and 1 tbsp oil, season with salt and pepper and leave to set.
Add couscous with tomatoes, cucumber, parsley (all diced), carrots (grated), chives and mint (finely chopped).
Season the couscous salad with lemon juice, salt and pepper.

9.36 Cream cheese substitute

Good to fight lactose intolerance. Strengthens body energy, promotes digestion, promotes weight loss. Good to fight immunodeficiency, loss of appetite, arteriosclerosis, flatulence, bladder weakness, anemia, high blood pressure, depressions, diabetes, diarrhea.
Cooking time approx. 20 min
Calories p. portion: 526
2 portions
Allergens: AE

Quantity of ingredients
Soybean milk 4 cup / 300g. (yes)
Lemon 1 piece / 50g. (yes)
Herbs various 2 table spoons / 6g. (yes)
Whole grain bread 6 slices / 300g. (recommended)

Cooking instructions:
Heat the soy milk in a saucepan till it boils, stirring occasionally (gets burn easily!), Then allow to cool.
Squeeze out the lemon and stir gently under the cooled soy milk (approx. 80°C/176°F), let it approx. 20 min. rest or clot.
Pour chopped soy milk through a strainer lined with a dishcloth, allow liquid to drain and then squeeze out remaining liquid with the dishcloth.
Refine to taste with fresh herbs.
Serve with wholemeal bread.

9.37 Cucumber salad

Diuretic, detoxifying, suppresses conversion of sugar into fat, lowers cholesterol, prevents cancer. Cucumber cools and moistens. Dill works against flatulence, anticonvulsant in gastrointestinal discomfort.
Cooking time approx. 5 min
Calories p. portion: 27
2 portions
Allergens: O

Quantity of ingredients
Cucumber 1 piece / 400g. (recommended)
Salt 1 pinch / 1g. (little)
Dill 1 pinch / 1g. (yes)
Vinegar (Apple vinegar) 1 table spoon / 10g. (yes)

Cooking instructions:
Cut the cucumber (do not peel the BIO) thinly and season.

9.38 Curdcheesedumplings on strawberry pulp

Strawberry forcing spleen and stomach, strengthens blood. Chicken egg calms nerves and stomach.
Cooking time approx. 30 min
Calories p. portion: 553
5 portions
Allergens: ACG

Quantity of ingredients
Curd cheese 20% 1,1 lbs / 500g. (recommended)
Spelled semolina 3/8 lbs - 6oz / 150g. (yes)
Butter organic 1/8 lbs - 2oz / 40g. (yes)
Chicken egg 2 pieces / 120g. (yes)
Sugar - icing sugar 2 table spoons / 20g. (little)
Salt 1 pinch / 1g. (little)
Breadcrumbs (wheat bread, bread roll) 2 table spoons / 25g. (yes)
Butter organic 1/4 lbs - 4oz / 100g. (yes)
Strawberries 1,1 lbs / 500g. (recommended)
Sugar - icing sugar 2 table spoons / 25g. (little)

Cooking instructions:
Curdcheese, grit, butter, eggs, powdered sugar and salt to a smooth dough. Keep the dough 15 mins in the refrigerator to settle down. Then shape small dumplings with a diameter of approx 4cm and boil them for about 10 minutes in slightly boiling salt water. Heat butter in a pan and roast the breadcrumbs golden brown. Roll the dumplings carefully into the crumbs.
Serve the dumplings with the strawberry.

9.39 Curry rice with raisins and nuts

Stops diarrhea, promotes digestion, appetizing, harmonizes the stomach, improves blood circulation, improves medication effect, stimulates appetite, detoxifies the skin, stimulates nerves, frees breathing, increases body temperature, promotes perspiration.
Cooking time approx. 30 min
Calories p. portion: 275
4 portions
Allergens: HO

Quantity of ingredients
Sunflower oil 1 table spoon / 15g. (yes)
Onion white 1 piece / 50g. (yes)
Curry 1/2 teaspoon / 2g. (yes)
Rice wild (nature rice) 1 cup / 120g. (recommended)
Salt 1 pinch / 1g. (little)
White wine 1/2 cup / 125g. (little)
Lemon Alternatively for white wine / g. (yes)
Peppers powder 1 pinch / 1g. (yes)
Apple (sweet) 2 pieces / 300g. (recommended)

Raisins 2 table spoons / 25g. (yes)
Walnuts 2 table spoons / 25g. (recommended)
Water 6 cups / 500g. (yes)

Cooking instructions:
Heat oil in a pot; fry chopped onions until glassy; add the curry and let it foam for a short time; then fry the raw rice for a few minutes over a gentle heat, stirring constantly; Salt, a dash of white wine or lemon juice, rose paprika, sweet apples chopped, raisins, chopped, roasted nuts added; pour hot water on it until well covered; simmer until the rice is cooked.

Goes well with: carrot and fennel vegetables, legumes with boiled vegetables, sliced poultry with ginger and mushrooms.

9.40 Duck with mung beans

Strengthens blood, forcing spleen, supports urination, promotes spleen and liver, reduces blood pressure, strengthens immune system, prevents cancer, reduces radiation damage, dissolves stagnation.
Cooking time approx. 2 hours
Calories p. portion: 747
5 portions
Allergens: E

Quantity of ingredients
Duck (slaughtered) 1/2 piece / 1250g. (yes)
Onion white 2 pieces / 120g. (yes)
Carrot 1 piece / 120g. (recommended)
Garlic 1 clove / 3g. (yes)
Mung bean 5/8 lbs - 8oz / 250g. (yes)
Peppercorns 3 pieces / 2g. (yes)
Honey 1 teaspoon / 3g. (yes)
Soy sauce 1 teaspoon / 3g. (yes)
Lemon juice 1 teaspoon / 3g. (yes)
Salt 1 pinch / 1g. (little)
Pepper (ground) 1 pinch / 0,5g. (yes)
Olive oil 1 table spoon / 10g. (yes)
Bay leaf 2 leaves / 2g. (yes)
Black caraway 1 pinch / 1g. (yes)
Savory 1 teaspoon / 2g. (recommended)

Cooking instructions:
The day before soak the mung beans and rinse the duck cold. Wash the vegetables, clean and cut into pieces. Put the duck and vegetables in a saucepan and cover with water. Add bay leaves, savory, mugwort and peppercorns. Boil over medium heat and simmer for 45 minutes. Skim off the foam. Remove duck from the stock, allow to cool and keep cool overnight.

In a saucepan, sauté the chopped onion in olive oil and pour in 1/4 liter of stock and add the pre-cooked vegetables. Add the mung beans and season with honey, soy sauce, lemon juice, salt, crushed black cumin and pepper.

Serve with rice or potatoes.

9.41 Fennel and potato gratin

Reduces inflammation, improves blood circulation, improves digestion, supports urination, lowers cholesterol, good to fight loss of appetite, flatulence, inflammatory bowel disease, heartburn. Forcing spleen, improves blood circulation.
Cooking time approx. 1 1/2 hours
Calories p. portion: 147
2 portions
Allergens: CGL

Quantity of ingredients
Fennel 5/8 oz / 200g. (recommended)
Potato 1/4 lbs - 4oz / 125g. (yes)
Basic recipe for a vegetable soup (nutritious) 1/2 cup / 100g. (yes)
Butter organic 1 teaspoon / 3g. (yes)
Rice flour 2 teaspoons / 6g. (yes)
Cream sour 10% 1 teaspoon / 3g. (yes)
Salt 1 pinch / 1g. (little)
Sugar cane sugar 1 pinch / 1g. (little)
Chicken yolk 1 piece / 10g. (little)
Pepper Cayenne 1 pinch / 0,5g. (yes)
Nutmeg 1 pinch / 0,5g. (yes)
Parsley 1 teaspoon / 2g. (yes)
Chives 1 teaspoon / 3g. (yes)
Parmesan 1 teaspoon / 3g. (yes)
Butter organic 1 teaspoon / 3g. (yes)

Cooking instructions:
Cook peeled potatoes and then let cool. Wash the fennel, cut off the stems and remove any outer leaves.
Hold back fennel greens and add it to the sauce with the other herbs later.
Steam the fennel tubers for about 15 - 20 minutes.
Then cut the potatoes and fennel into slices and place in layers in a greased baking dish.
Bring the liquid of fennel broth to the boil and bind it with flour.
Season with sea salt, cayenne pepper, sugar, nutmeg and sour cream.
Allow to cool and alloy with egg yolk.
Spread the sauce over the casserole, sprinkle with parmesan and finely chopped parsley and chives. Bake at 200 °C / 392 °F in the oven for half an hour.

9.42 Figs with mozzarella and honey

Promotes digestion, reduces inflammation, bloating and nausea, relaxing and reassuring, relieves pain, detoxifying, blood stilling, forcing spleen and digestive system, detoxifying, bactericide.
Cooking time approx. 10 min
Calories p. portion: 415
1 portions
Allergens: GO

Quantity of ingredients
Fig 4 pieces / 100g. (yes)
Mozzarella 1 piece / 50g. (yes)
Basil (fresh) 1/2 bunch / 50g. (yes)
Honey 2 table spoons / 24g. (yes)
Pepper (ground) 1 pinch / 0,1g. (yes)
Grapeseed oil 1 table spoon / 12g. (yes)
Vinegar Aceto Balsamico white 1 table spoon / 12g. (yes)

Cooking instructions:
Quarter fresh figs, dice buffalo mozzarella, pluck basil leaves.
Mix a dressing with light balsamic vinegar, grapeseed oil and honey and season to taste.
Place the figs on the edge of the appropriate plate. Spread the mozzarella cubes and season with black pepper.
Spread whole or roughly sliced basil leaves over it and moisten with the marinade.
Spiced pizza bread goes perfectly with it.

9.43 Fine Russian borscht

Strengths spleen and stomach, strengthens the heart, stimulates digestion, reduces blood pressure, strengthens immune system. For strengthening after diseases. Good to fight bloating, cramping in gastrointestinal complaints.
Cooking time approx. 30 min
Calories p. portion: 172
6 portions
Allergens: AGLO

Quantity of ingredients
Red beet 5/8 oz / 200g. (recommended)
Sunflower oil 1 table spoon / 10g. (yes)
Onion (shallot) 2 pieces / 40g. (yes)
Carrot 2 pieces / 140g. (recommended)
Celery root 1 piece / 500g. (recommended)
Parsley root 1 piece / 150g. (yes)
Leek 1/8 lbs - 2oz / 50g. (yes)
Basic recipe for a vegetable soup (nutritious) 3 cups / 650g. (yes)
Bay leaf 1 Leaf / 0,2g. (yes)
Juniper berry 2 pieces / 2g. (recommended)
Nutmeg 1 pinch / 1g. (yes)
Savoy cabbage / kale 5/8 oz / 200g. (recommended)
Salt 1 pinch / 1g. (little)
Pepper (ground) 1 pinch / 0,5g. (yes)
Ground 1 pinch / 1g. (yes)
Red wine 1/2 cup / 125g. (little)
Sour cream 15% fat 1 table spoon / 10g. (yes)
Dill 1 teaspoon / 10g. (yes)
White bread (wheat bread) 6 slices / 120g. (little)

Cooking instructions:
Fry some beetroot in oil. Fry the onions, carrots, celery, parsley root and leek well in another pan. Add the stock and the wine; then add bay leaves, juniper berries and nutmeg and simmer for 15 minutes. Remove the bay leaf and puree everything.
Heat more broth separately, simmer the steamed beetroot in it. Add cabbage or white cabbage after half the cooking time and let it steep. At the end, add the pureed vegetables and season with salt, pepper, ground cumin and a little red wine. Garnish with some sour cream and finely chopped dill in the plate. Serve with a slice of white bread.

9.44 Fish soup with rosemary

Promotes spleen and liver, reduces blood pressure, strengthens immune system, has little cholesterol and is protein rich, improves blood circulation, increases appetite. Antioxidant, dissolves stagnation.
Cooking time approx. 30 min
Calories p. portion: 271
4 portions
Allergens: DLO

Quantity of ingredients
Basic recipe for a fish soup 2 cup / 500g. (yes)
Rosemary 1/2 bunch / 7g. (yes)
Onion (spring onion) 1 piece / 20g. (yes)
Olive oil 2 table spoons / 35g. (yes)
Fish pieces mixed (fresh water) 5/8 lbs - 8oz / 250g. (recommended)
Carrot 1 piece / 120g. (recommended)
Parsnip 1 piece / 180g. (yes)
Celery root 1 slice / 20g. (recommended)
Salt 1 pinch / 1g. (little)
Peppercorns 2 pieces / 1g. (yes)
Garlic 1 clove / 3g. (yes)

Cooking instructions:
Fry the onion and garlic in oil. Add fish broth. Add diced carrots, parsnips and celery. Season with salt and peppercorns. Simmer the soup on a low heat for 25 minutes.
Wash the fish, drizzle with lemon juice, divide into pieces and add to the soup with the pink rosemary. Cook for 5 min on low heat.
Add the chives and parsley and season the soup with the salt.

9.45 Grapefruit juice

Promotes digestion, lowers blood glucose, dries out, provides Vitamin C
Cooking time approx. 5 min
Calories p. portion: 107
1 portions
Allergens:

Quantity of ingredients
Grapefruit (Pomelo) 1 cup / 250g. (yes)

Cooking instructions:
Juice fresh grapefruit or use organic juice.

9.46 Grilled tomatoes with cheese filling

Promotes digestion, helps to digest fat, supports urination, reduces blood pressure, stimulates digestion.
Cooking time approx. 30 min
Calories p. portion: 470
2 portions
Allergens: ACG

Quantity of ingredients
Tomato 8 pieces / 200g. (recommended)
Feta cheese 0,2 lbs / 75g. (yes)
Fresh cheese 0,2 lbs / 75g. (yes)
Chicken egg 1 piece / 60g. (yes)
Olive oil 1 table spoon / 12g. (yes)
Basil (fresh) 1 table spoon / 6g. (yes)
Salt 1 pinch / 1g. (little)
Pepper (ground) 1 pinch / 0,5g. (yes)
Olives 1 oz / 30g. (yes)
Rucola 1/4 lbs / 100g. (recommended)
White bread (wheat bread) 4 slices / 80g. (little)

Cooking instructions:
Hollow out tomatoes generously. Put in a casserole dish.
Mix cheese, olive oil, egg, chopped basil and flour. Season with salt and pepper and fill in the tomatoes.
Bake in the preheated oven at 210 degrees on the middle rail for 15 minutes, then switch on the oven grill and grill for a further 3 minutes (without circulating air).
Stone the olives and chop and sprinkle on the tomatoes.
Garnish tomatoes with rocket and serve with white bread.

9.47 Halibut with tomato and garlic sauce

Promotes digestion, helps to digest fat, supports urination, reduces blood pressure, good to fight rheumatism, flatulence, bladder weakness, anemia, high blood pressure, depressions, diabetes, diarrhea. Valuable omega-3 fatty acids.
Cooking time approx. 45 min
Calories p. portion: 319
5 portions
Allergens: D

Quantity of ingredients
Rice variety any 1 cup / 120g. (yes)
Water 6 cups / 240g. (yes)
Salt 1 pinch / 1g. (little)
Halibut (Flatfish) 2,2 lbs / 800g. (yes)
Salt 1 pinch / 1g. (little)
Pepper (ground) 1 pinch / 0,5g. (yes)
Lemon juice 1 dash / 2g. (yes)
Bay leaf 2 pieces / 2g. (yes)
Lemon 1 piece / 30g. (yes)
Garlic 8 pieces / 10g. (yes)
Thyme dried 1 table spoon / 5g. (yes)
Olives 0,2 lbs / 75g. (yes)
Tomato 4 pieces / 200g. (recommended)
Salt 1 pinch / 1g. (little)
Pepper (ground) 1 pinch / 0,5g. (yes)

Cooking instructions:
Cook rice with salted water (1:3).
Rinse the fish under running cold water, dab with kitchen paper and rub
with salt, pepper and lemon juice.
Place the fish fillets in a casserole dish with pieces of bay leaf.

Wash the lemon hot and cut into slices, peel and halve the garlic.
Sprinkle the olives and the thyme over them.
Brew the tomatoes with hot water, skin and chop.

Mix all ingredients, season with salt and pepper and distribute around
the fish.

Cook everything at 200°C/392°F for about 20 minutes.
Serve with the rice.

9.48 Hearty polenta mash

Strengths spleen and stomach, promotes watering, promotes digestion,
detoxifying, promotes perspiration, reduces blood lipids, stimulates,
dissolves stagnation, stimulates appetite, dissolves stagnation.
Cooking time approx. 10 min
Calories p. portion: 262
2 portions
Allergens:

Quantity of ingredients
Corn Grease (Polenta) 1 cup / 120g. (yes)
Onion (spring onion) 2 pieces / 40g. (yes)
Ginger fresh 1/2 teaspoon / 2g. (yes)
Nutmeg 1 pinch / 1g. (yes)
Salt 1 pinch / 1g. (little)
Olive oil 1 table spoon / 10g. (yes)
Turmeric (yellow root) 1 pinch / 1g. (yes)
Water 1 1/2 cups / 240g. (yes)

Cooking instructions:
Stir in the polenta in boiling water and let it swell for 7 min. Add green onion, grated ginger, turmeric, nutmeg, salt and olive oil and wait for 3 more minutes.

9.49 Hearty winter breakfast

Strengthens immune system, calms nerves and stomach, promotes digestion, detoxifying, strengthens bodily production, promotes perspiration, reduces blood lipids, stimulates, dissolves stagnation.
Cooking time approx. 20 min
Calories p. portion: 678
1 portions
Allergens: ACEG

Quantity of ingredients
Oat meal 1 cup / 120g. (yes)
Ginger fresh 1/2 teaspoon / 1g. (yes)
Salt 1 pinch / 1g. (little)
Onion (spring onion) 2 pieces / 40g. (yes)
Chicken egg 1 piece / 55g. (yes)
Butter organic 1 table spoon / 15g. (yes)
Soy sauce 1 dash / 3g. (yes)

Cooking instructions:
Soak oatmeal overnight. Boil in the morning with a little ginger, salt and a spring onion or leek and then let it swell until the porridge is soft. Before serving, add a whole egg to the porridge, add the butter and season to taste with a little soy sauce.

Recommendation: Especially suitable for the cold season.

9.50 Hungarian rice salad

Promotes digestion, helps to digest fat, supports urination, reduces blood pressure, strengthens kidney and bladder, diuretic, warming the body from the inside, expands blood vessels, strengthens the muscles, regulates internal organs functions.
Cooking time approx. 25 min
Calories p. portion: 421
2 portions
Allergens: GM

Quantity of ingredients
Rice (whole grain) 1/2 cup / 60g. (recommended)
Water 3 cups / 300g. (yes)
Salt 1 pinch / 0,3g. (little)
Tomato 1/4 lbs - 4oz / 100g. (recommended)
Peppers 1/8 lbs - 2oz / 50g. (recommended)
Champignon 1 oz / 30g. (yes)
Edam cheese 1 oz / 30g. (yes)
Yogurt (natural, 1.5% fat) 1/8 lbs - 2oz / 45g. (recommended)
Salt 1 pinch / 1g. (little)
Herbs various 1 table spoon / 8g. (yes)
Rapeseed oil 2 table spoons / 20g. (recommended)
Mustard 1 teaspoon / 3g. (yes)
Pepper (ground) 1 pinch / 0,2g. (yes)

Cooking instructions:
Pour the rice into plenty of boiling salt water and let it drain gently. Wash tomatoes and peppers and core. Cut both in to small cubes. Peel the mushrooms (from the tin or with rapeseed oil for a short time) and cut the cheese into small cubes and add to the rice. Prepare the marinade and mix with the ingredients, refrigerate and leave for at least an hour.

9.51 Lasagne with tofu cream

Harmonizes spleen and stomach, reduces Flatulence, protects the digestive system. Good to fight lack of appetite, flatulence, inflammatory bowel disease, stomach ulcers, rheumatism, heartburn, twelffinger intestinal ulcers.
Cooking time approx. 45 min
Calories p. portion: 301
4 portions
Allergens: ACEG

Quantity of ingredients
Soy Tofu 7/8 lbs / 400g. (yes)
Chicken egg 2 pieces / 100g. (yes)
Onion white 2 pieces / 120g. (yes)
Tomato 1/4 lbs - 4oz / 100g. (recommended)
Oregano dried 1 pinch / 1g. (yes)
Marjoram 1 pinch / 1g. (yes)
Peppers powder 1 pinch / 1g. (yes)
Salt 1 pinch / 1g. (little)
Noodles (wheat, lasagne) with egg 3/8 lbs - 6oz / 150g. (yes)
Edam cheese 1/8 lbs - 2oz / 50g. (yes)

Cooking instructions:
Tofu cream: Mix tofu with eggs, onions, small tomatoes, oregano, marjoram, peppers and some sea salt put into a smooth mass using a kitchen machine with a knife or a blender.

Lasagne: Place 1/5 of the tofu cream in a casserole dish (25x15cm), cover with 3 lasagna leaves, repeat this process twice, and then finish the last fifth of the tofu cream over the pastry plates. Sprinkle with a little grated
Edam and bake in the oven at 175°C/347°F for about 1/2 hour.

9.52 Leek and potato gratin

Reduces inflammation, improves digestion, regenerates skin, supports urination, lowers cholesterol, promotes sweating, dissolves stagnation.
Cooking time approx. 1 hour
Calories p. portion: 368
4 portions
Allergens: CGL

Quantity of ingredients
Potato 1,1 lbs / 500g. (yes)
Leek 1,1 lbs / 500g. (yes)
Apple (sour) 1 piece / 200g. (recommended)
Créme fraiche cheese 1/4 lbs - 4oz / 125g. (yes)
Basic recipe for a vegetable soup (nutritious) 1/4 cup / 20g. (yes)
Chicken yolk 1 piece / 20g. (little)
Emmental cheese 2 table spoons / 20g. (yes)
Salt 1 pinch / 1g. (little)
Pepper (ground) 1 pinch / 0,5g. (yes)

Cooking instructions:
Wash the potatoes, peel, cut into very thin slices and pat dry. Place half in a flat greased baking dish.
Clean and wash leeks and cut into fine rings. Wash apple, peel and cut into thin slices. Spread the leek rings and apple slices on top. Put the remaining potato slices on top.
Mix crème fraiche, egg yolk, grated Emmentaler, salt and pepper, if necessary add some vegetable stock and pour over the casserole.
Bake at 200°C/392°F in the oven for about 45 to 50 minutes until golden brown. Cover with parchment paper after 30 minutes to prevent the burr from drying out.

9.53 Lettuce with fresh cheese

The bitter substances have diuretic effect and promote the blood circulation in the digestive area. Mustard improves thyroid function, relieves rheumatism symptoms.
Cooking time approx. 5 min
Calories p. portion: 802
1 portions
Allergens: AFM

Quantity of ingredients
Leaf salads (bitter) 2 portions / 60g. (recommended)
Fresh cheese from soya 3/8 lbs - 6oz / 150g. (yes)
Mustard 1 knife tip / 1g. (yes)
Lemon juice 1 dash / 3g. (yes)
Salt 1 pinch / 1g. (little)
Pepper (ground) 1 pinch / 0,5g. (yes)
Herbs various 2 teaspoons / 4g. (yes)
Black caraway 1 pinch / 1g. (yes)
Whole grain bread 2 slices / 40g. (recommended)

Cooking instructions:
Wash lettuce and finely pluck.
Mix 150 ml cream cheese, splashes of mustard, splashes of lemon juice, 1 clove of garlic, chopped fresh herbs, pinch of pepper and crushed black cumin and pour over. Serve with wholemeal bread.

9.54 Lettuce with vinegar dressing

Relieves fatigue, regulates gastrointestinal function, dissolves stagnation, laxative, antiparasitic, improves blood circulation, detoxifying, reduces inflammation, relieves pain.
Cooking time approx. 10 min
Calories p. portion: 68
2 portions
Allergens: O

Quantity of ingredients
Lettuce 1 piece / 200g. (recommended)
Vinegar (Apple vinegar) 1 table spoon / 10g. (yes)
Water 1 table spoon / 10g. (yes)
Rapeseed oil 1 table spoon / 10g. (recommended)
Onion (spring onion) 1 piece / 20g. (yes)
Salt 1 pinch / 0,5g. (little)
Pepper (ground) 1 pinch / 0,1g. (yes)
Chives 1 table spoon / 5g. (yes)

Cooking instructions:
Clean lettuce, wash and drain. Add the ingredients to the marinade in an extra container. Salad with marinade just before consumption. Just before, sprinkle with chives.

9.55 Mango banana yoghurt drink ice cold

Good to fight loss of appetite, oral mucosa inflammation. Regulates gastrointestinal function, chronic constipation. Prevents cancer.
Diuretic, forcing spleen.
Cooking time approx. 5 min
Calories p. portion: 121
2 portions
Allergens: G

Quantity of ingredients
Mango juice 1/2 cup / 100g. (yes)
Yogurt (natural, 1.5% fat) 1/4 lbs - 4oz / 100g. (recommended)
Mineral water 1/2 cup / 100g. (yes)
Banana 1/2 piece / 150g. (yes)
Acerola fruit nectar or powder 1 teaspoon / 2g. (yes)

Cooking instructions:
Mix all the ingredients and 2-3 ice cubes in a blender.

9.56 Marinated cod on pumpkin puree

Reduces inflammation, improves digestion, promotes spleen, lung, stomach and kidneys, diuretic, reduces blood glucose, good to fight constipation and flatulence, dissolves stagnation.
Cooking time approx. 2 hours
Calories p. portion: 202
4 portions
Allergens: DG

Quantity of ingredients
Potato 6 pieces / 400g. (yes)
Pumpkin 5/8 oz / 200g. (yes)
Onion white 1 piece / 50g. (yes)
Oregano dried 1/2 teaspoon / 1g. (yes)
Lemon juice 1/2 piece / 15g. (yes)
Salt 1 pinch / 1g. (little)
Pepper (ground) 1 pinch / 0,3g. (yes)
Créme fraiche cheese 2 table spoons / 30g. (yes)
Yogurt (natural, 1.5% fat) 3/8 lbs - 6oz / 150g. (recommended)
Oregano dried 1/4 teaspoon / 1g. (yes)
Basil (fresh) 1/2 teaspoon / 2g. (yes)
Cod 3/4 lbs / 300g. (recommended)
Salt 1 pinch / 1g. (little)
Pepper (ground) 1 pinch / 0,3g. (yes)
Olive oil 1 teaspoon / 3g. (yes)

Cooking instructions:
Mix yoghurt with oregano, basil and thyme.
Wash the fish fillets, pat dry, place in a flat shape and pour over the marinade. Leave 2 hours in refrigerator.

Cook the potatoes in salted water until soft and peel.

Sauté the onion in oil until glassy, add the diced pumpkin and cook for about 10 min. Add oregano, lemon juice, salt, pepper and crème fraiche and puree with the blender.

Remove fish fillets from the marinade, drain, pat dry and salt. Coat a coated grill pan with 2 teaspoons of oil. Roast the fish fillets on both sides for 3 - 4 minutes and arrange with the potatoes on the pumpkin puree.

9.57 Millet with pears

Refreshing and nourishing, promotes digestion, supports urination, good to fight cough, promotes perspiration, reduces blood lipids, stimulates, dissolves stagnation, forces liver, strengthens the muscles, lowers cholesterol, antiparasitic.
Cooking time approx. 35 min
Calories p. portion: 213
5 portions
Allergens: G

Quantity of ingredients
Millet 1 cup / 120g. (yes)
Water 1 1/2 cups / 200g. (yes)
Grape juice red 1 1/2 cups / 240g. (yes)
Pear 4 pieces / 600g. (recommended)
Ginger fresh 1/2 teaspoon / 2g. (yes)
Salt 1 pinch / 1g. (little)
Acerola fruit nectar or powder 1 teaspoon / 2g. (yes)
Cocoa 1 pinch / 1g. (yes)
Sunflower seeds 2 table spoons / 4g. (yes)
Barley malt 1/2 teaspoon / 2g. (yes)
Cream, sweet 30% 2 teaspoons / 20g. (little)

Cooking instructions:
Simmer the millet for 5 min and let it swell for another 30 min.

Then: In a hot pot, heat some grape juice; add chopped pears, very little grated ginger, a pinch of salt, acerola, a pinch of cocoa and sauté briefly; add the boiled millet, sunflower seeds, some barley malt to taste, 1 tsp cream per serving or a little butter.

9.58 Noodles with turkeymeat and pineapple

Solves bile-, kidney- and bladder stones, provides Vitamin C, strengthens blood, strengthens bone marrow, reduces inflammation, supports urination.
Cooking time approx. 45 min
Calories p. portion: 292
4 portions
Allergens: ACGL

Quantity of ingredients
Noodles (whole grain) with egg 5/8 oz / 200g. (recommended)
Pineapple 5/8 oz / 200g. (yes)
Water 1/2 cup / 50g. (yes)
Turkey breast meat 5/8 oz / 200g. (recommended)
Rapeseed oil 1 table spoon / 12g. (recommended)
Garlic 1 piece / 2g. (yes)
Basic recipe for a vegetable soup (nutritious) 1/2 cup / 100g. (yes)
Cow's milk (whole milk 3.5% fat) 2/3 cup / 180g. (yes)
Fresh cheese 0,2 lbs / 75g. (yes)
Curry 3 teaspoons / 6g. (yes)
Salt 1 pinch / 1g. (little)
Pepper (ground) 1 pinch / 0,5g. (yes)
Pomegranate 1 piece / 300g. (yes)
Coconut flakes 1 table spoon / 6g. (yes)

Cooking instructions:
Cook the noodles in salt water. Cut the pineapple into cubes and leave
for 5 min. to simmer in water. Cut the meat sliced in strips and roast
them in the oil. Add the chopped garlic and the pineapple sliced. Add
about 50 ml of the ananas juice and stir in the vegetable broth. Add the
milk and the fresh cheese, then stir well until the fresh cheese is
completely dissolved. Now add the curry and simmer for a few minutes
until a creamy consistency is reached.
Season with salt and pepper. Now add the noodles in the finished
sauce. Cut the pomegranate and release the seeds. Distribute as many
kernels on the dressed noodles. Whoever likes it can spread coconut
chips over it.

9.59 Noodles with vegetable and tomato sauce

Protects the digestive system. Detoxifying, Good to fight loss of
appetite, flatulence, inflammatory bowel disease, obesity, gout, stomach
ulcers, stomach cramps, rheumatism, heartburn, twelffinger intestinal
ulcers, promotes digestion, helps to digest fat.
Cooking time approx. 45 min
Calories p. portion: 562
2 portions
Allergens: ACG

Quantity of ingredients
Tomato 1/4 lbs - 4oz / 125g. (recommended)
Carrot 1 piece / 80g. (recommended)
Zucchini 1 piece / 80g. (recommended)
Olive oil 1 table spoon / 15g. (yes)
Onion (shallot) 1 piece / 20g. (yes)
Oregano dried 1 pinch / 1g. (yes)
Salt 1 pinch / 1g. (little)
Pepper (ground) 1 pinch / 0,2g. (yes)
Noodles (wheat) with egg 5/8 oz / 200g. (yes)
Olive oil 1 table spoon / 10g. (yes)
Créme fraiche cheese 2 table spoons / 30g. (yes)

Cooking instructions:
Boil the tomatoes with a little water, drain and collect the juice, cut the tomatoes into pieces.
Roughly grate zucchini and carrot. Heat olive oil in a pot. Steam shallots very soft. Add tomatoes, season with oregano, salt and pepper. Simmer tomatoes to a thick sauce.
Bring plenty of salted water to boil, cook the wholegrain noodles until firm.
In the cooking time of the pasta, heat in a pan olive oil. Fry the carrots while stirring, lightly salt. Add zucchini, sauté briefly while stirring. The vegetables should be soft with a bite.
Drain pasta, mix with créme fraiche, season with salt and pepper.
Garnish with the tomato sauce.

9.60 Oat flakes with aromatic spices

Stops diarrhea, promotes digestion, appetizing, harmonizes the stomach, relieves diarrhea, strengthens immune system, detoxifying and stimulating the immune system.
Cooking time approx. 25 min
Calories p. portion: 280
3 portions
Allergens: AH

Quantity of ingredients
Oat flakes (whole grain) 1 cup / 125g. (recommended)
Walnuts 1 table spoon / 15g. (recommended)
Hazelnuts 1 table spoon / 15g. (yes)
Water 1 1/2 cups / 240g. (yes)
Wakame 1 inch / 2g. (yes)

Apple (sweet) 1 piece / 220g. (recommended)
Cardamom 3-4 capsules / 2g. (yes)
Lemon Balm (fresh) 3-4 leaves / 3g. (yes)
Acerola fruit nectar or powder 1 teaspoon / 2g. (yes)

Cooking instructions:
Roast oatmeal and nuts. Add hot water. Add cardamom, wakame and cook for 20 min. Add grated apple, acerola and lemon herb.

9.61 Oriental rice pan

Forcing spleen, dissolves stagnation, promotes weight loss. Good to fight immunodeficiency, loss of appetite, flatulence, high blood pressure, helps to digest fat, strengthens kidney and bladder.
Numerous vitamins, minerals and secondary plant active ingredients.
Cooking time approx. 30 min
Calories p. portion: 303
6 portions
Allergens: EL

Quantity of ingredients
Rice (whole grain) 3/8 lbs - 6oz / 180g. (recommended)
Basic recipe for a vegetable soup (nutritious) 2 1/4 cups / 500g. (yes)
Curry 1/2 teaspoon / 2g. (yes)
Onion (spring onion) 4 pieces / 80g. (yes)
Rapeseed oil 2 table spoons / 20g. (recommended)
Peppers 1/4 lbs - 4oz / 120g. (recommended)
Corn 3 oz / 80g. (yes)
Shiitake, dried 1/2 oz / 80g. (yes)
Bamboo shoots 3 oz / 80g. (yes)
Peas 3 oz / 80g. (yes)
Peaches 1/8 lbs - 2oz / 60g. (recommended)
Pineapple 1/8 lbs - 2oz / 60g. (yes)
Tomato 5/8 oz / 200g. (recommended)
Lovage 1 teaspoon / 2g. (yes)
Basil (fresh) 1 teaspoon / 2g. (yes)
Parsley 1 teaspoon / 2g. (yes)
Lemon Balm (fresh) 1 teaspoon / 2g. (yes)
Pepper (ground) 1 pinch / 1g. (yes)

Cooking instructions:
Soak the mushrooms in water 20 min.
Boil the rice in the vegetable stock 15 min. and season with some curry.
Peel the onion, cut into fine cubes.
Heat the oil in a pan and sauté the onion cubes.
Wash the peppers in half, remove the core, cut into cubes and add.
Add corn, mushrooms and bamboo shoots, simmer 5 min. until firm.
Also add the bean sprouts, peas, peach cubes and pineapple cubes.
Then add the peeled, chopped tomatoes.
Add the cooked rice and season with the herbs and pepper.

9.62 Oven potatoes with celery-curd cheese (quark)

Promotes spleen, reduces Inflammation, improves digestion,
regenerates skin, supports urination, lowers cholesterol.
Cooking time approx. 30 min
Calories p. portion: 304
2 portions
Allergens: GL

Quantity of ingredients
Celery root 3 oz / 80g. (recommended)
Basic recipe for a vegetable soup (nutritious) 1/2 cup / 100g. (yes)
Ground caraway 1 pinch / 0,2g. (yes)
Lemon peel 1/2 teaspoon / 1g. (yes)
Salt 1 pinch / 1g. (little)
Pepper (ground) 1 pinch / 0,2g. (yes)
Lemon juice 1 teaspoon / 3g. (yes)
Curd cheese 20% 5/8 oz / 200g. (recommended)
Créme fraiche cheese 1/2 teaspoon / 5g. (yes)
Potato 6 pieces / 400g. (yes)
Olive oil 2 teaspoons / 5g. (yes)
Salt 1 pinch / 1g. (little)

Cooking instructions:
Celery-curd cheese:
Mix celery with vegetable broth according to basic recipe, caraway and
lemon peel. Cook for about 8 minutes until the celery is soft and the
vegetable broth almost evaporated. Mix the celery vegetable broth with
the lemon juice, finely, and stir until smooth. Season with salt and
pepper.
Baked potatoes:
Preheat oven to 200 °C / 400 °F.

Brush the potatoes well, halve them, and place them on a baking tray with the cut surface facing up. Lightly salt the surfaces and sprinkle with oil. Fry the potatoes in the oven for about 25 minutes.
Serve the celery plug to the potatoes.

9.63 Oyster mushrooms with asparagus

Forces, reduces inflammation, improves digestion, lowers cholesterol, strengthens kidney, stimulates liver function, improves blood circulation, improves medication effect, increases appetite.
Cooking time approx. 30 min
Calories p. portion: 316
4 portions
Allergens: GH

Quantity of ingredients
Onion white 1 piece / 50g. (yes)
Butter organic 2 table spoons / 40g. (yes)
Oyster mushroom 3/4 lbs / 300g. (yes)
Sake 2 table spoons / 40g. (yes)
Parsley 2 table spoons / 40g. (yes)
Walnuts 2 table spoons / 60g. (recommended)
Asparagus (green or white) 1,1 lbs / 500g. (recommended)
Salt 1 pinch / 1g. (little)
Sugar white 1 pinch / 0,1g. (little)
Potato 1 lbs / 500g. (yes)
Salt (herbal) 1 pinch / 1g. (yes)

Cooking instructions:
Cook organically grown potatoes with the skin, otherwise prepare peeled boiled potatoes. Boil the asparagus in salted water with a pinch of sugar and salt. (You can cook an old roll that absorbs the bittering substances.)
Slightly sauté the chopped onions in a pan in the butter before frying the oyster mushrooms cut into the same pan.
Stew 15 minutes, stirring several times. Add the sake, walnuts and parsley and simmer on low heat while you drain the potatoes and asparagus. Finally, sprinkle some herbal salt over it.
If no fresh asparagus is available, asparagus can be used in jars.

9.64 Pancakes with spinach and parmesan

Promotes bowel movement, improves blood circulation, forcing spleen and bowel, strengthens immune system, good to fight loss of appetite, flatulence, high blood pressure, depressions, diabetes, constipation, inflammatory bowel disease
Cooking time approx. 25 min
Calories p. portion: 330
6 portions
Allergens: ACGL

Quantity of ingredients
Wholemeal flour 1/4 lbs - 4oz / 100g. (recommended)
Wheat flour 1/4 lbs - 4oz / 100g. (yes)
Chicken egg 4 pieces / 200g. (yes)
Cow's milk (whole milk 3.5% fat) 1 1/2 cups / 400g. (yes)
Salt 1 pinch / 1g. (little)
Sunflower oil 1 table spoon / 15g. (yes)
Olive oil 1 table spoon / 15g. (yes)
Onion white 1 piece / 50g. (yes)
Parsley 1/2 bunch / 80g. (yes)
Basic recipe for a vegetable soup (nutritious) 1/2 cup / 150g. (yes)
Basil (fresh) 1/4 teaspoon / 1g. (yes)
Nutmeg 1 pinch / 0,3g. (yes)
Créme fraiche cheese 2 table spoons / 45g. (yes)
Spinach 1,3 lbs / 600g. (yes)
Salt 1 pinch / 1g. (little)
Pepper (ground) 1 pinch / 0,1g. (yes)
Parmesan 1/8 lbs - 2oz / 60g. (yes)

Cooking instructions:
Stir flour, eggs and milk and a pinch of salt with the whisk until smooth. From the dough, fry pancakes crispy brown on both sides.

Heat oil in a small saucepan. Fry the finely chopped onion until tender. Stir in chopped parsley, sauté briefly. Add the vegetable broth according to the basic recipe, season with basil and nutmeg. Cover and simmer for 15 minutes, add crème fraiche and finely puree.
Cook the washed, drizzled spinach with a little salt in a closed pan over a moderate heat in 3 minutes, drain in a sieve and cut into small pieces. Add the spinach to the sauce, heat briefly. Add parmesan in the mix.
Fill the pancakes with the cream spinach.

9.65 Plum Cake

Cancer preventive effect, dehydrates the body, stimulates digestion and binds fats in the intestine, good to fight loss of appetite, flatulence, inflammatory bowel disease, obesity, gout, stomach ulcers, stomach cramps, rheumatism, heartburn. Relieves pain, detoxifying, bactericide.
Cooking time approx. 1 hour
Calories p. portion: 502
6 portions
Allergens: AG

Quantity of ingredients
Curd cheese 20% 5/8 oz / 200g. (recommended)
Wheat flour 7/8 lbs / 400g. (yes)
Cow's milk (whole milk 3.5% fat) 6 table spoons / 70g. (yes)
Rapeseed oil 6 table spoons / 70g. (recommended)
Honey 8 table spoons / 100g. (yes)
Baking powder 1 package / 3g. (yes)
Salt 1 pinch / 1g. (little)
Cinnamon ground 1 teaspoon / 3g. (yes)
Plums 2,2 lbs / 1000g. (recommended)

Cooking instructions:
Mix the flour, curd cheese, milk, oil, honey, salt and baking powder into a smooth dough. Keep the dough cool for 15 minutes to cool.
Lay out baking paper on a baking sheet and press the dough out to a bottom.
Now spread the plums evenly.
Sprinkle the cake with the cinnamon and bake for about 40 minutes at 190 ° C/374 °F.

9.66 Polenta with fried egg

Calms nerves, forcing spleen and stomach, lets urine and bile juice flow, prevents cancer, forcing spleen, improves blood circulation, encourages growth, dissolves stagnation.
Cooking time approx. 15 min
Calories p. portion: 410
2 portions
Allergens: CG

Quantity of ingredients
Water 1 1/2 cups / 200g. (yes)
Corn Grease (Polenta) 1 cup / 120g. (yes)
Ginger fresh 1 pinch / 0,5g. (yes)
Butter organic 1/2 teaspoon / 2g. (yes)
Pepper (ground) 1 pinch / 0,2g. (yes)
Nutmeg 1 pinch / 0,2g. (yes)
Salt 1 pinch / 0,5g. (little)
Lemon juice 1 dach / 1g. (yes)
Pepper powder (hot) 1 pinch / 0,3g. (yes)
Chicken egg 4 pieces / 250g. (yes)
Chives 2 table spoons / 14g. (yes)

Cooking instructions:
Stir in a saucepan with hot water polenta and a little ginger; swell until
the polenta is cooked.
Add a piece of butter, pepper, nutmeg, salt, a few drops of lemon, a
pinch of rose paprika.
Put the polenta in a fireproof bowl.
Put 1 fried egg per person on top; bake in the oven for a few minutes,
so that the egg yolk is still liquid.
Sprinkle with ground pepper, finely chopped chives and a little salt.

9.67 Polenta with peach

Relieves fatigue, forcing spleen, diuretic, strengthens the defense, good
to fight fungi infections, lets urine and bile juice flow, prevents the aging
process, strengthens brain cells.
Cooking time approx. 20 min
Calories p. portion: 197
3 portions
Allergens:

Quantity of ingredients
Water 1 1/2 cups / 240g. (yes)
Corn Grease (Polenta) 1 cup / 120g. (yes)
Peaches 2-3 pieces / 400g. (recommended)
Vanilla pod 1 pinch / 1g. (yes)
Cinnamon ground 1 pinch / 1g. (yes)

Cooking instructions:
Pour the polenta into a pan of hot water with constant stirring until the
polenta has the desired consistency. Pull the polenta from the fire and

let it soak for 10 minutes.
Wash fresh peaches and cut into quarters. Pour into the finished polenta the peaches, add the vanilla and add Chili to taste, stir and let it go for 3 minutes.
Winter varieties: Pickled fruit, pear, apples

9.68 Potato bags with wild herbs and tomato sauce

Promotes spleen, improves digestion, good to fight loss of appetite, flatulence, inflammatory bowel disease, prostate disorders.
Cooking time approx. 45 min
Calories p. portion: 418
5 portions
Allergens: ACG

Quantity of ingredients
Olive oil 1 table spoon / 10g. (yes)
Onion white 1 piece / 50g. (yes)
Garlic 1 piece / 2g. (yes)
Tomato puree 7/8 lbs / 400g. (yes)
Salt 1 pinch / 1g. (little)
Pepper (ground) 1 pinch / 0,5g. (yes)
Cream, sweet 30% 1 table spoon / 10g. (little)
Potato 1,4 lbs / 650g. (yes)
Wheat flour 5/8 oz / 200g. (yes)
Chicken egg 1 piece / 60g. (yes)
Salt 1 pinch / 1g. (little)
Pepper (ground) 1 pinch / 0,5g. (yes)
Nutmeg 1 pinch / 0,2g. (yes)
Nettles 1/8 lbs - 2oz / 50g. (yes)
Dandelion (young plants) 1 oz / 30g. (yes)
Yarrow 1 oz / 30g. (yes)
Chervil dried 1/2 oz / 10g. (yes)
Ribworttea 1/2 oz / 10g. (yes)
Parsley 1/8 lbs - 2oz / 50g. (yes)
Olive oil 1 table spoon / 10g. (yes)
Garlic 1 piece / 2g. (yes)
Curd cheese 20% 4 table spoons / 40g. (recommended)
Mayonnaise 50% 1 table spoon / 10g. (little)
Salt (herbal) 1/2 teaspoon / 2g. (yes)
Black caraway 1 pinch / 1g. (yes)
Pepper (ground) 1 pinch / 0,5g. (yes)
Emmental cheese 1/4 lbs / 100g. (yes)

Cooking instructions:
Tomato sauce:
Heat oil. Roast diced onion briefly with crushed garlic. Add the tomato puree and let it thicken for 2 minutes while stirring, season with salt and pepper and add the cream and place in a fireproof mold.

Potato Batter:
Cook the boiled potato, drain, peel and squeeze. Mix in a bowl with flour, Parmesan, egg and spices. Roll out the dough on a lightly floured work surface and cut into 5 cm squares.

Herb Stuffing:
Chop the herbs and mix with oil, garlic, curd cheese, mayonnaise, herb salt, crushed black cumin and pepper to a creamy mass.

Put on the pastry with a spoon in the middle. Fold into a triangle, press on the edge and let the pockets soak in plenty of salted water until they float up. Add to the tomatoes, sprinkle with the grated cheese and bake in the oven until golden brown.

9.69 Potato cream with herbs and fresh cheese

Good to fight loss of appetite, constipation, bloating and nausea.
Improves digestion, supports urination, prevents cancer, forcing spleen, dissolves stagnation, relaxing and reassuring.
Cooking time approx. 25 min
Calories p. portion: 217
2 portions
Allergens: G

Quantity of ingredients
Potato (mealy) 5/8 lbs - 8oz / 250g. (yes)
Fresh cheese 3 oz / 80g. (yes)
Yogurt (natural, 1.5% fat) 2 table spoons / 45g. (recommended)
Chives 1/2 bunch / 50g. (yes)
Basil (fresh) 1 teaspoon / 4g. (yes)
Parsley 1 teaspoon / 4g. (yes)
Dill 1/2 teaspoon / 2g. (yes)
Salt 1 pinch / 1g. (little)
Black caraway 1 pinch / 0,5g. (yes)
Pepper (ground) 1 pinch / 0,5g. (yes)

Cooking instructions:
Softly steam the potatoes in the pan, peel them and press through the potato press.
Mix cream cheese, yoghurt and herbs under the potatoes, season with salt, crushed black cumin and pepper.

9.70 Potato gnocchi with vegetables and basil sauce

Strengthens immune system, promotes weight loss. Good to fight immunodeficiency, loss of appetite, flatulence, high blood pressure. Relaxing and reassuring.
Cooking time approx. 1 hour
Calories p. portion: 167
4 portions
Allergens: ACGL

Quantity of ingredients
Potato 5/8 lbs - 8oz / 250g. (yes)
Wheat flour 1 oz / 25g. (yes)
Wheat semolina 1/2 oz / 15g. (yes)
Chicken yolk 1 piece / 20g. (little)
Nutmeg 1 pinch / 0,2g. (yes)
Basic recipe for a vegetable soup (nutritious) 1 cup / 250g. (yes)
Celery root 1/8 lbs - 2oz / 50g. (recommended)
Lemon peel 1/2 teaspoon / 2g. (yes)
Ginger fresh 1/2 teaspoon / 2g. (yes)
Nutmeg 1 pinch / 0,2g. (yes)
Basil (fresh) 1 Bunch / 125g. (yes)
Créme fraiche cheese 1 table spoon / 20g. (yes)
Salt 1 pinch / 1g. (little)
Pepper (ground) 1 pinch / 0,2g. (yes)
Carrot 1/4 lbs - 4oz / 100g. (recommended)
Zucchini 1/4 lbs - 4oz / 100g. (recommended)
Cauliflower 1/4 lbs - 4oz / 100g. (recommended)
Broccoli 1/4 lbs - 4oz / 100g. (recommended)
Salt 1 pinch / 1g. (little)

Cooking instructions:
Steam the potatoes gently, peel and pass hot through the potato press.
Process the hot potatoes with flour, semolina, egg, nutmeg and salt to a smooth dough. Let dough rest for 3o minutes.
Make small rolls (2 cm) out of the dough with flour-dusted hands, cut off 1 cm thin slices. To create the typical gnocchi shape, gently dab the

dough pieces with your thumb. Leave the gnocchi in lightly boiling salted water for 6 - 8 minutes. Lift the gnocchi out of the pot with the skimmer.

Heat the vegetable stock till it boils. Add diced celery, grated lemon peel, finely chopped ginger and 1 pinch of nutmeg. Cover and simmer for about 10 minutes. Using the blender, puree the vegetable broth, celery, chopped basil and créme fraiche into a smooth sauce. Season with salt and nutmeg.

Cut carrots, zucchini, cauliflower and broccoli into small pieces and cook covered in a sieve over steam for 8 minutes until firm.
Heat the sauce again and add to the vegetables and arrange over the gnocchi.

9.71 Potatoes with wild garlic-curd cheese

Improves digestion, regenerates skin, supports urination, lowers cholesterol. Helps to fight stomach pressure, belching, diabetes, acute or chronic constipation of the intestine. Improves the flow characteristics of the blood.
Cooking time approx. 20 min
Calories p. portion: 254
2 portions
Allergens: G

Quantity of ingredients
Potato 3/4 lbs / 300g. (yes)
Salt 1 pinch / 0,1g. (little)
Wild garlic (garlic spinach) 2 handful / 30g. (yes)
Curd cheese 20% 5/8 lbs - 8oz / 250g. (recommended)
Yogurt (natural, 1.5% fat) 2 table spoons / 20g. (recommended)
Salt 1 pinch / 1g. (little)

Cooking instructions:
Cook potatoes in salted water and peel.
Wash he wild garlic leaves and carefully dried and cut into fine strips.
Mix the cottage cheese, yogurt and salt and mix in the chopped wild garlic pieces. Serve with the potatoes.
In the season in which no wild garlic grows the wild garlic pesto can be used.

9.72 Pumpkin soup

Promotes digestion, forcing spleen and stomach, reduces blood pressure, strengthens immune system, prevents cancer, reduces radiation damage, improves digestion, regenerates skin, lowers cholesterol, reduces blood glucose, protects liver.
Cooking time approx. 1 hour
Calories p. portion: 105
3 portions
Allergens:

Quantity of ingredients
Pumpkin 3/4 lbs / 300g. (yes)
Carrot 2 pieces / 100g. (recommended)
Potato 2 pieces / 120g. (yes)
Olive oil 1 table spoon / 10g. (yes)
Onion white 1 piece / 50g. (yes)
Water 1 cup / 120g. (yes)
Parsley 1 table spoon / 7g. (yes)
Anise (Common Fennel) 1 pinch / 1g. (yes)
Salt 1 pinch / 1g. (little)

Cooking instructions:
Add the olive oil to the pan, add the diced pumpkin, diced carrots and potatoes. Roast them shortly, add the finely chopped onion, fill with water, add enough water to cover the vegetables at least 3 finger-widths. Boil at low heat.

Season with sea salt, add small cutted parsley, a pinch of anise (little).

Allow to simmer for about 35 minutes. Then purée the soup and add some water, depending on the consistency of the soup.

9.73 Rhubarb and apple jelly

Antioxidants, lots of vitamin C, laxative, relieves pain, detoxifying, warms stomach and spleen, improves blood circulation.
Cooking time approx. 15 min
Calories p. portion: 180
2 portions
Allergens:

Quantity of ingredients
Rhubarb 5/8 oz / 200g. (recommended)
Apple juice (natural cloudy) 1 cup / 300g. (yes)
Corn starch 1 oz / 30g. (yes)
Honey 1/2 oz / 20g. (yes)
Vanilla sugar natural 1 pinch / 0,5g. (yes)
Cinnamon ground 1 pinch / 0,5g. (yes)
Peppermint 2 leaves / 2g. (yes)

Cooking instructions:
Add the cornstarch to a 1/2 cup apple juice.
Simmer the rhubarb in 1 cup of water for 10 min.
Add the remaining apple juice and the cornstarch, stir, heat till it boils again.
Sweet with honey and season with vanilla and cinnamon. Spread the mixture on dessert bowls and garnish with mint.

9.74 Rhubarb cake with sprinkles

Laxative, antipyretic. Protects the digestive system. Detoxifying, affects anorexia, good to fight flatulence, inflammatory bowel disease, brittle nails and hair. Relieves pain, detoxifying, against dry skin, acne, eczema.
Cooking time approx. 1 1/2 hours
Calories p. portion: 476
8 portions
Allergens: AG

Quantity of ingredients
Wheat flour 7/8 lbs / 400g. (yes)
Cow's milk (whole milk 3.5% fat) 1 cup / 200g. (yes)
Yeast 1 oz / 30g. (yes)
Honey 2 teaspoons / 5g. (yes)
Sunflower oil 2 teaspoons / 5g. (yes)
Lemon peel 1 piece / 3g. (yes)
Salt 1 pinch / 1g. (little)
Rhubarb 2,2 lbs / 800g. (recommended)
Margarine 1/4 lbs - 4oz / 120g. (yes)
Wheat flour 3/4 lbs / 300g. (yes)
Vanilla sugar natural 2 pinches / 1g. (yes)
Cinnamon ground 2 pinches / 1g. (yes)
Honey 5 table spoons / 50g. (yes)

Cooking instructions:
Mix flour, grated lemon peel and salt.
Heat milk gently and mix with yeast and honey.
Then add the flour mixture and the oil and knead vigorously. Cover the
dough and let it rise in a warm place until it reaches twice the amount.
(about 30 minutes)

For the sprinkles, mix flour with vanilla and cinnamon, then add honey
and margarine and crumble to a crumbly mass. Keep the sprinkles
dough cool.

Lay out a baking sheet with parchment paper.
Knead the dough for the bottom again, roll it out, place it on the baking
sheet and let it rise for another 10 minutes.

Clean the rhubarb, wash it, halve lengthwise and cut into pieces of
approx. 3 cm. Spread the pieces on the rolled out dough and crumble
the sprinkles over the cake.

Place the cake in the preheated oven at 175 ° C and bake for about 40
minutes.

9.75 Rice congee with honey pear and black sesame

Promotes digestion, supports urination, good to fight blood circulation
disorders, thromboses, risk of embolism, high blood pressure, a
headache, heart attack and stroke.
Cooking time approx. 10 min - 3 hours
Calories p. portion: 158
2 portions
Allergens: N

Quantity of ingredients
Basic recipe for a rice soup (Congee) 1 1/2 cups / 240g. (yes)
Pear 2 pieces / 300g. (recommended)
Sesame, black 1 teaspoon / 3g. (yes)

Cooking instructions:
Cook rice congee according to basic recipe.
Fill pot with 3 cm of water and heat till it boils. Quarter the pears (with
the skin and seeds) and simmer them covered with black sesame for 10
minutes. Mix with the rice.

9.76 Rice with stewed vegetables

Reduces blood pressure, strengthens immune system, prevents cancer, reduces radiation damage, extremely low fat content, good to fight blood circulation disorders, thrombose, risk of embolism, a headache, heart attack and stroke. Is diuretic.
Cooking time approx. 20 min
Calories p. portion: 166
2 portions
Allergens: L

Quantity of ingredients
Rice variety any 1/2 cup / 60g. (yes)
Water 3 cups / 300g. (yes)
Lemon peel 1 piece / 3g. (yes)
Water 1/2 cup / 0g. (yes)
Carrot 2 pieces / 180g. (recommended)
Celery sticks 1/2 piece / 5g. (recommended)
Champignon 1/2 cup / 50g. (yes)
Cress 2 table spoons / 20g. (yes)
Linseed oil 1 dash / 3g. (recommended)

Cooking instructions:
Cook rice according to basic recipe with a piece of lemon peel.
Steam chopped carrots, celery and mushrooms until soft.
Then sprinkle with cress. Then add a dash of high quality cold oil.

9.77 Roasted millet with plum compote

Supports urination, promotes spleen and kidney, strengthens the defense. Good to fight fungi infections.
Cooking time approx. 30 min
Calories p. portion: 139
4 portions
Allergens:

Quantity of ingredients
Millet 1 cup / 120g. (yes)
Water 1 1/2 cups / 250g. (yes)
Plum 1 1/2 cups / 250g. (recommended)
Vanilla pod 1 pinch / 1g. (yes)
Water 5/8 lbs - 8oz / 250g. (yes)
Cinnamon ground 1 pinch / 1g. (yes)
Acerola fruit nectar or powder 1/2 teaspoon / 1g. (yes)

Cooking instructions:
Roast millet briefly, pour over water, heat till it boils and let stand for 20 min. to swell.

Cook plums with water, vanilla and cinnamon 10 min. then strain. Add acerola and add to the millet.

9.78 Rosemary Potatoes

Reduces Inflammation, improves digestion, regenerates skin, supports urination, lowers cholesterol. Rosemary stimulates digestion, strengthens lung, promotes spleen and kidney, dries out.
Cooking time approx. 30 min
Calories p. portion: 188
2 portions
Allergens:

Quantity of ingredients
Potato 6-8 pieces / 420g. (yes)
Salt (herbal) 1 pinch / 1g. (yes)
Olive oil 1 table spoon / 10g. (yes)
Rosemary 1 teaspoon / 2g. (yes)

Cooking instructions:
Cut the potatoes into half´s, apply a little olive oil on the cut surface, then salt, sprinkle 2 - 3 rosemary needles on the potatoes.
Place the potatoes on the baking tray and bake them in the preheated oven for approx. 25 minutes to 190°C/374°F.

9.79 Salmon on tomato-spinach

Promotes bowel movement, improves blood circulation, forcing spleen and bowel, strengthens blood, reduces inflammation, improves digestion, regenerates skin, supports urination, lowers cholesterol, promotes sweating, dissolves stagnation.
Cooking time approx. 1 hour
Calories p. portion: 365
6 portions
Allergens: D

Quantity of ingredients
Potato 1,1 lbs / 500g. (yes)
Salt 1 pinch / 1g. (little)
Salmon 1,3 lbs / 600g. (recommended)
Rapeseed oil 2 teaspoons / 24g. (recommended)
Tomato 1/4 lbs - 4oz / 100g. (recommended)
Spinach 1,5 lbs / 700g. (yes)
Salt 1 pinch / 1g. (little)
Pine nuts 4 table spoons / 40g. (yes)
Leek 1/4 lbs - 4oz / 120g. (yes)
Olive oil 4 table spoons / 40g. (yes)
Salt 1 pinch / 1g. (little)
Pepper white (ground) 1 pinch / 0,5g. (yes)

Cooking instructions:
Peel the potato and cut into cubes, cook in salted water.
Cut the salmon into portions and fry slowly and evenly in a frying pan
from both sides, seasoned with salt and pepper, then add the pine nuts
and lightly roast.
Blanch spinach in salted water.
Lightly sweat the finely chopped leek with a little rapeseed oil, add the
blanched spinach and heat evenly.
Just before serving, add the halved cocktail tomatoes to the spinach
and season the vegetables well with salt and pepper.
Arrange the spinach and leek tomato bed with the potatoes, add the
salmon and sprinkle with the salted pine nuts.
Drizzle with a little olive oil and serve the dish.

9.80 Scrambled eggs with rocket and herbs

Calms nerves and stomach, promotes digestion, detoxifying,
strengthens bodily fluids production, promotes perspiration, reduces
blood lipids, stimulates, dissolves stagnation, stimulates liver function,
harmonizes liver and spleen, strengthens eyesight, detoxifying.
Cooking time approx. 10 min
Calories p. portion: 360
1 portions
Allergens: CG

Quantity of ingredients
Butter organic 2 table spoons / 20g. (yes)

Ginger fresh 1 knife tip / 1g. (yes)
Chicken egg 2 pieces / 120g. (yes)
Pepper (ground) 1 pinch / 0,5g. (yes)
Coriander 1 pinch / 1g. (yes)
Parsley 2 table spoons / 16g. (yes)
Rucola 2 handful / 30g. (recommended)
Oregano dried 1 teaspoon / 2g. (yes)
Savory 1 pinch / 0,5g. (recommended)

Cooking instructions:
Melt a piece of butter in a hot pan; add fine cutted ginger and roast it
shortly. Mix in 1 egg whipped, pepper freshly ground, a pinch of
coriander, bean cabbage, some salt, parsley chopped, rocket and
oregano cut into small pieces until the egg stalls, but still juicy.
Garnish: millet, polenta, potatoes, toasted bread. The dish is
wholesome, without carbohydrate.

9.81 Semolina porridge with banana

Regulates gastrointestinal function, reduces inflammation, antiallergic,
good to fight blood circulation disorders.
Cooking time approx. 15 min
Calories p. portion: 307
1 portions
Allergens: AG

Quantity of ingredients
Cow's milk (whole milk 3.5% fat) 3/4 cup - 6 oz / 200g. (yes)
Spelled semolina 2 table spoons / 30g. (yes)
Butter organic 1 teaspoon / 4g. (yes)
Banana 1/2 piece / 50g. (yes)

Cooking instructions:
Heat the half of the milk in a small pot. Add the semolina and boil it
shortly in the milk. Let it swell at low heat for 3 minutes with constant
stirring. Remove the pot from the heat, add the remaining milk with the
snow bean and place the mush in a small bowl. Add the butter and the
battered banana.
For adults, a pinch of cinnamon can be spread over it.

9.82 Sliced chicken with walnuts and sherry

Strengthens blood, strengthens bone marrow, strengthens gastrointestinal function, expands blood vessels, prevents cancer, promotes perspiration, reduces blood lipids, stimulates.
Cooking time approx. 25 min
Calories p. portion: 304
4 portions
Allergens: EGHN

Quantity of ingredients
Butter organic 2 table spoons / 35g. (yes)
Walnuts 2 table spoons / 25g. (recommended)
Ginger fresh 1/2 teaspoon / 2g. (yes)
Onion (shallot) 2 pieces / 40g. (yes)
Salt 1 pinch / 1g. (little)
Chicken meat 3/4 lbs / 300g. (yes)
Peppers powder 1 pinch / 1g. (yes)
Sesame, white 1 teaspoon / 2g. (yes)
Black fungus mushroom 4 pieces / 3g. (yes)
Shiitake, dried 4 pieces / 5g. (yes)
Soy sauce 1 dash / 3g. (yes)
Rice (whole grain) 1 cup / 120g. (recommended)
Water 6 cups / 550g. (yes)
Salt 1 pinch / 1g. (little)

Cooking instructions:
Heat butter or sesame oil in a hot pan; Sauté walnuts, copious grated ginger, chopped shallots or onions; Add the salt and the sliced chicken and sauté everything; Rose paprika, roasted sesame, soaked black fungus, shiitake mushrooms or mushrooms; with a shot sherry; infuse with water; Simmer for 5 to 10 minutes until the meat is cooked; Season with soy sauce.

Place the rice in salted water, heat till it boils and let it simmer over low heat for about 15 minutes.

This fits: lamb's lettuce, Radicchio

9.83 Spelled with fruit and nuts

Stops diarrhea, promotes digestion, appetizing, relieves fatigue, anti-inflammatory (gastrointestinal). Good to fight tumor lesions and leukemia, is antiallergic in food allergies, regulates metabolism, lowers blood glucose and cholesterol.
Cooking time approx. 1 1/2 hours
Calories p. portion: 290
3 portions
Allergens: AH

Quantity of ingredients
Spelled grain 1 cup / 120g. (yes)
Water 1 cup / 50g. (yes)
Apple (sweet) 1 piece / 220g. (recommended)
Apricot 1 piece / 200g. (yes)
Peaches 1 piece / 120g. (recommended)
Cinnamon ground 1 pinch / 1g. (yes)
Cardamom 1 pinch / 1g. (yes)
Salt 1 pinch / 1g. (little)
Strawberries 1 cup / 120g. (recommended)
Almond puree 1 table spoon / 15g. (yes)
Cocoa 1 pinch / 1g. (yes)
Walnuts 1 table spoon / 10g. (recommended)

Cooking instructions:
Put spelled in hot water and cook.

Then: Give sweet chopped fruit (apples, apricots, peaches) in a little hot water, with a little cinnamon, sauté briefly; ground cardamom and / or coriander, a small pinch of salt, the boiled spelled, berries after season. Put some cocoa and roasted nuts over it.

9.84 Spicy avocado cream with cottage cheese

Anti-inflammatory, good to fight swelling, pain and itching, forcing spleen and digestive system, detoxifying, bactericide.
Cooking time approx. 15 min
Calories p. portion: 614
4 portions
Allergens: G

Quantity of ingredients
Avocado 2 pieces / 600g. (yes)
Pepper (ground) 1 pinch / 0,5g. (yes)
Salt 1 pinch / 1g. (little)
Lemon juice 1/2 piece / 15g. (yes)
Peppers powder 1 pinch / 1g. (yes)
Olive oil 1 table spoon / 10g. (yes)
Herbs various 1 table spoon / 7g. (yes)
Cottage cheese 1 cup / 250g. (yes)
Bread with carob kernel flour 8 slices / 200g. (yes)

Cooking instructions:
Peel, core and purée avocados; add plenty of ground pepper, salt,
lemon juice, rose paprika, a few drops of oil, chili, fresh chopped herbs,
a pinch of salt; cottage cheese (about the same amount as avocado
cream), carefully submerge.

Goes well with: Potatoes and millet, with which the avocado cream in
combination with vegetable dishes, legumes or lettuce leaves a
delicious meal. It is also very good as an appetizer, as a souvenir at
parties and as a morning meal in the summer together with a mild dish
of lentils or Adzuki beans and grated radish.

9.85 Spicy cake with dates

Good to fight loss of appetite, flatulence, inflammatory bowel disease,
obesity, gout, stomach ulcers, stomach cramps, rheumatism, heartburn.
Calms nerves and stomach, improves blood circulation.
Cooking time approx. 1 1/2 hours
Calories p. portion: 808
4 portions
Allergens: ACGO

Quantity of ingredients
Sunflower oil 1/2 cup / 100g. (yes)
Sugar white 5/8 oz / 200g. (little)
Cow's milk (whole milk 3.5% fat) 1/2 cup / 100g. (yes)
Wheat flour 5/8 lbs - 8oz / 250g. (yes)
Cocoa 1/8 lbs - 2oz / 40g. (yes)
Dates dried 1/8 lbs - 2oz / 50g. (yes)
Chicken egg 3 pieces / 180g. (yes)
Clove 1/2 teaspoon / 1g. (yes)
Cinnamon ground 1 1/2 tea spoon / 3g. (yes)

Nutmeg 1 pinch / 0,5g. (yes)
Baking powder 1/2 package / 1,5g. (yes)
Butter organic 1 teaspoon / 2g. (yes)
Wheat flour 1 teaspoon / 2g. (yes)

Cooking instructions:
Separate eggs. Stir egg whites until stiff and set aside.
Add oil, sugar, egg yolk to a bowl and stir until frothy.
Add the flour, cocoa and baking powder, stir. Stir in the milk. Now add
the minced dates and the spices (the cloves as grated powder) to the
mixture and mix with low speed of the hand mixer.
Now, take the stiffly egg white spoonful carefully under.
Put the dough in a greased, floured mold and bake at 200°C/392°F for
70 minutes.

9.86 Strawberry yoghurt and almond puree mix

Relieves pain and inflammation in rheumatism. Good to fight acute or
chronic constipation of the intestine. Little laxative. Relieves pain,
detoxifying, bactericide.
Cooking time approx. 5 min
Calories p. portion: 134
3 portions
Allergens: GH

Quantity of ingredients
Yogurt (natural, 1.5% fat) 5/8 oz / 200g. (recommended)
Strawberries 1,5 lbs / 700g. (recommended)
Honey 1 teaspoon / 3g. (yes)
Acerola fruit nectar or powder 1 teaspoon / 2g. (yes)
Almond puree 2 teaspoons / 6g. (yes)

Cooking instructions:
Puree yoghurt, strawberries, acerola, honey and almond paste in a
blender.

9.87 Sugar pea soup with prawns

Reduces blood pressure, strengthens immune system, forcing spleen,
lets lymph flow.
Cooking time approx. 15 min
Calories p. portion: 215
3 portions
Allergens: BL

Quantity of ingredients
Peas 5/8 lbs - 8oz / 250g. (yes)
Basic recipe for a vegetable soup (nutritious) 2 cup / 500g. (yes)
Olive oil 1 teaspoon / 3g. (yes)
Onion (spring onion) 1 piece / 20g. (yes)
Parsley 1 Bunch / 15g. (yes)
Olive oil 1 teaspoon / 3g. (yes)
Shrimp 8 pieces / 120g. (yes)
Salt 1 pinch / 0,5g. (little)
Pepper (ground) 1 pinch / 0,1g. (yes)

Cooking instructions:
Cook the peas in a saucepan with water until soft, strain and quench
with cold water. Mince the parsley, add to the peas and pour in the
vegetable broth. Chop onions and fry in a little olive oil, add to soup and
puree. Sauté the prawns in olive oil, cut into bite-sized pieces and add
to the soup. Season with salt and pepper.

9.88 Tea from anise

Anise (wild fennel) promotes digestion, forcing spleen and stomach.
Cooking time approx. 15 min
Calories p. portion: 3
4 portions
Allergens:

Quantity of ingredients
Anise (Common Fennel) 1 teaspoon / 3g. (yes)
Water 2 cup / 500g. (yes)

Cooking instructions:
Heat the water till it boils and put it aside. Add anise.
10 min. to let go.
Pour through a tea strainer. Sweet to taste with honey.

In order to achieve a salutary effect, you should drink 2 cups of anise
tea per day.

9.89 Tea from chamomile

Good to fight flatulence, nausea, intestinal cramps, diarrhea, inflammation of the oral mucosa, influenza infections, stomach and intestinal mucosa infections, badly healing wounds, nausea, colds, skin rashes, inflammation in the genital and anal area.
Cooking time approx. 10 min
Calories p. portion: 0
1 portions
Allergens:

Quantity of ingredients
Chamomile 1 teaspoon / 3g. (yes)
Water 1 cup / 120g. (yes)

Cooking instructions:
Heat the water till it boils and put it aside. Chamomile flowers added and 10 min. to let go.

9.90 Tea Green tea

Green tea promotes digestion, supports urination, dissolves mucus, detoxifying, stimulates nerves, reduces blood lipids, lowers cholesterol, reduces inflammation.
Cooking time approx. 10 min
Calories p. portion: 2
1 portions
Allergens:

Quantity of ingredients
Green tea 1 teaspoon / 2g. (yes)
Water 1 cup / 120g. (yes)

Cooking instructions:
For each cup you use a teaspoonful or a teabag.
Pour green tea only with 60 to 80 ° C / 140 to 176 °F hot water, otherwise it will be bitter.
If the tea has a stimulating effect, let it draw for two to three minutes. It has a calming effect for a duration of five minutes (no longer, otherwise it will be bitter!).
Another method: Pour the tea leaves with about 70 ° C / 158 °F hot water and pour the water immediately again.
Then just pour hot water again. The bitter substances disappear and the tea gets a milder aroma.

9.91 Tomato soup

Promotes digestion, helps to digest fat, supports urination, reduces blood pressure, dissolves stagnation. Contains unsaturated fatty acids, is antioxidativ.
Cooking time approx. 10 min
Calories p. portion: 100
2 portions
Allergens:

Quantity of ingredients
Olive oil 1 table spoon / 15g. (yes)
Onion white 1 piece / 60g. (yes)
Cinnamon ground 1 pinch / 1g. (yes)
Basil (fresh) 1 teaspoon / 2g. (yes)
Pepper (ground) 1 pinch / 0,5g. (yes)
Salt 1 pinch / 1g. (little)
Tomato 6 pieces / 250g. (recommended)
Water 5/8 lbs - 8oz / 250g. (yes)
Peppers powder 1 pinch / 1g. (yes)

Cooking instructions:
Roast the onion in a pot. Salt and spices. Briefly roast. Put washed and quartered tomatoes in the pan. Stir and sauté briefly. Add a quart of water and heat till it boils. Cook for a quarter of an hour and puree.

9.92 Tomato with mozzarella

Promotes digestion, helps to digest fat, supports urination, reduces blood pressure. Affects anorexia, good to fight flatulence, inflammatory bowel disease, bloating and nausea. Relaxing and reassuring.
Cooking time approx. 5 min
Calories p. portion: 436
1 portions
Allergens: AG

Quantity of ingredients
Mozzarella 1 piece / 50g. (yes)
Tomato 2 pieces / 100g. (recommended)
Salt 1 pinch / 1g. (little)
Basil (fresh) 5 leaves / 6g. (yes)
Olive oil 2 table spoons / 20g. (yes)
White bread (wheat bread) 2 slices / 40g. (little)

Cooking instructions:
Cut tomatoes and mozzarella into slices. Serve with salt, basil and olive oil. Serve with white bread.

9.93 Vanilla cream with berries

Weakness, chronic constipation of the intestine, weight loss, laxative, detoxifying, blood detoxifying.
Strengthens the defense. Good to fight fungi infections.
Cooking time approx. 15 min
Calories p. portion: 278
4 portions
Allergens: G

Quantity of ingredients
Curd cheese 20% 7/8 lbs / 400g. (recommended)
Yogurt (natural, 1.5% fat) 3/8 lbs - 6oz / 150g. (recommended)
Sugar brown 2 teaspoons / 8g. (little)
Acerola fruit nectar or powder 1 teaspoon / 2g. (yes)
Vanilla sugar natural 3 package / 3g. (yes)
Cream (30% fat) 1/4 lbs - 4oz / 125g. (little)
Strawberries 1/4 lbs - 4oz / 100g. (recommended)
Raspberry 1/4 lbs - 4oz / 100g. (recommended)
Blackberry´s 1/4 lbs - 4oz / 100g. (recommended)
Blueberry 1/4 lbs - 4oz / 100g. (yes)

Cooking instructions:
Mix the curd cheese, yoghurt, sugar, acerola and vanilla sugar with a hand mixer or whisk until smooth. Beat the whipped cream very stiff, mix it under the cream. Arrange vanilla cream in portions with the berries.

9.94 Vegetable bowl with tofu and curry on rice

Diuretic, reduces blood glucose. Reduces flatulence, supports digestion. Contains ideal herbal mucus, which provides regeneration of the small and large intestinal flora. Reduces blood pressure, strengthens immune system.
Cooking time approx. 30 min
Calories p. portion: 162
6 portions
Allergens: E

Quantity of ingredients
Olive oil 2 table spoons / 20g. (yes)
Garlic 2 cloves / 3g. (yes)
Onion white 1 piece / 60g. (yes)
Curry 2 table spoons / 16g. (yes)
Water 2 cup / 500g. (yes)
Turnips 2 pieces / 50g. (recommended)
Pumpkin 1 piece / 400g. (yes)
Carrot 1 piece / 100g. (recommended)
Parsnip 1 piece / 150g. (yes)
Potato 1 piece / 70g. (yes)
Sweet potato 1 piece / 70g. (yes)
Cauliflower 1/4 piece / 250g. (recommended)
Broccoli 1/2 piece / 250g. (recommended)
Okra 12 pieces / 200g. (yes)
Soy Tofu 1 piece / 250g. (yes)
Basil 2 table spoons / 12g. (yes)
Salt 1 pinch / 0,5g. (little)

Cooking instructions:
Heat the oil at medium temperature in a large, heavy casserole, add the garlic and onion and sauté with constant stirring. Sprinkle curry powder over it, fry gently for about 5 minutes and make sure that the garlic and curry do not burn. Add the water and heat till it boils. Gradually peel all vegetables, dice and add, starting with the varieties that need the longest cooking time. Once the water has boiled again, reduce the heat and simmer the vegetables for about 15 minutes. When it is almost soft. Add the cauliflower and broccoli florets and the okra and cook the stew for another 10 to 15 minutes. Add the tofu during the last 5 minutes.

Cook the brown rice at the same time: Sprinkle the rice in a medium saucepan with water, salt and cover for about 20 minutes. cook on a low heat. Take from the fire and another 10 min. to let go.

Arrange the stew over the brown rice and sprinkle with basil.

9.95 Vegetable juice

Promotes digestion, helps to digest fat, supports urination, reduces blood pressure, strengthens immune system, prevents cancer, reduces radiation damage, forcing spleen, is stimulating.
Cooking time approx. 15 min
Calories p. portion: 64

1 portions
Allergens: L

Quantity of ingredients
Celery root 1/2 oz / 20g. (recommended)
Carrot 1/4 lbs - 4oz / 100g. (recommended)
Tomato 1/4 lbs - 4oz / 100g. (recommended)
Garlic 1 piece / 2g. (yes)
Salt 1 teaspoon / 2g. (little)
Acerola fruit nectar or powder 1/2 teaspoon / 1g. (yes)

Cooking instructions:
Peel all ingredients and use the juicer to make a drink. Stir in the acerola.

9.96 Vegetable rice

Forcing spleen, dissolves stagnation, promotes weight loss. Good to fight immunodeficiency, loss of appetite, flatulence, high blood pressure, strengthens kidney and bladder. Diuretic, warming the body from the inside, regulates internal organs functions.
Cooking time approx. 30 min
Calories p. portion: 304
3 portions
Allergens: L

Quantity of ingredients
Broccoli 1/8 lbs - 2oz / 50g. (recommended)
Carrot 1/8 lbs - 2oz / 50g. (recommended)
Kohlrabi 1/8 lbs - 2oz / 50g. (recommended)
Cauliflower 1 oz / 30g. (recommended)
Peas 1/2 oz / 20g. (yes)
Margarine 1 teaspoon / 4g. (yes)
Rice (whole grain) 5/8 oz / 200g. (recommended)
Basic recipe for a vegetable soup (nutritious) 7/8 lbs / 400g. (yes)
Parsley 1/2 oz / 20g. (yes)
Pepper (ground) 1 pinch / 0,2g. (yes)

Cooking instructions:
Cut the broccoli, carrots and kohlrabi into small cubes, divide the cauliflower into small florets. Heat the margarine in a pan or saucepan, sauté the vegetables. Then add the rice, top up with the vegetable stock and leave to soak for 15-20 minutes.

In the meantime finely chop the parsley. After cooking, season the rice with freshly ground pepper and parsley.

9.97 Vegetable semolina soup

Diuretic, harmonizes the stomach and intestines, conducts bowel winds, reduces blood pressure, lowers cholesterol, detoxifying, good to fight loss of appetite, flatulence, inflammatory bowel disease, heartburn, twelffinger intestinal ulcers. Stimulates digestion, reduces pain.
Cooking time approx. 20 min
Calories p. portion: 199
3 portions
Allergens: AEGL

Quantity of ingredients
Basic recipe for a vegetable soup (nutritious) 2 cup / 500g. (yes)
Potato 1 piece / 80g. (yes)
Parsnip 1 piece / 180g. (yes)
Carrot 1 piece / 120g. (recommended)
Celery root 3/8 lbs - 6oz / 150g. (recommended)
Kohlrabi 1/2 piece / 200g. (recommended)
Beans (green, fresh) 1/4 lbs / 100g. (recommended)
Wheat semolina 2 table spoons / 24g. (yes)
Lovage 1/2 teaspoon / 2g. (yes)
Butter organic 1 table spoon / 20g. (yes)
Soy sauce 1 teaspoon / 3g. (yes)

Cooking instructions:
Worm the prepared vegetable soup; cook the vegetables in the soup softly. Spread some wheatgrass and let it swell. At the end, add lovage-green and a little butter and taste with soy sauce.

9.98 Vitamin drink

Regulates gastrointestinal function, promotes spleen and liver, reduces blood pressure, strengthens immune system, prevents cancer, reduces radiation damage, supports urination, quenches thirst, calms the stomach, prevents cancer.
Cooking time approx. 5 min
Calories p. portion: 172
3 portions
Allergens:

Quantity of ingredients
Orange juice 1 cup / 300g. (yes)
Carrot 5/8 oz / 200g. (recommended)
Banana 2 pieces / 300g. (yes)
Kiwi 1 piece / 20g. (yes)

Cooking instructions:
Chop oranges, carrots, bananas and kiwi and finely puree with the blender.

9.99 Warming carrot soup

Strengthens and warms, reduces blood pressure, strengthens immune system, prevents cancer, reduces radiation damage, strengthens gastrointestinal function.
Cooking time approx. 30 min
Calories p. portion: 133
3 portions
Allergens: HL

Quantity of ingredients
Carrot 4 pieces / 250g. (recommended)
Walnut oil 2 table spoons / 20g. (yes)
Onion (shallot) 2 pieces / 40g. (yes)
Anise (Common Fennel) 1/2 teaspoon / 1g. (yes)
Nutmeg 1 pinch / 1g. (yes)
Ginger fresh 1/2 teaspoon / 1g. (yes)
Salt 1 pinch / 1g. (little)
Basic recipe for a vegetable soup (nutritious) 2 cup / 500g. (yes)
Parsley 1 table spoon / 10g. (yes)

Cooking instructions:
Heat walnut oil in a hot pot and fry onions; steam the carrots in it; add anise, nutmeg, a little ginger, salt and sauté everything; add water or vegetable- or meat stock; cook everything soft and then puree; fold in parsley at the end.

Recommendation: Suitable for the cold season, especially if you use meat broth as a liquid for infusion.

9.100   Yogurt with honey and nuts

Relieves pain, detoxifying, promotes wound healing. Good to fight acute or chronic constipation of the intestine. Dissolves stones.
Cooking time approx. 5 min
Calories p. portion: 258
1 portions
Allergens: GH

Quantity of ingredients
Yogurt (natural, 3.5% fat) 1/4 lbs - 4oz / 125g. (yes)
Honey 2 table spoons / 30g. (yes)
Walnuts 1 table spoon / 12g. (recommended)

Cooking instructions:
Mix yoghurt with honey and finely chopped nuts.

9.101   Zucchini with basil pesto

Good to fight bloating and nausea. Relaxing and reassuring, promotes digestion, forcing spleen and digestive system, detoxifying, strengthens the muscles and bones, diuretic, supports urination, dissolves stagnation.
Cooking time approx. 25 min
Calories p. portion: 468
3 portions
Allergens: ACGHL

Quantity of ingredients
Basil (fresh) 1 Bunch / 125g. (yes)
Olive oil 1 table spoon / 20g. (yes)
Almond 1 table spoon / 15g. (yes)
Parmesan 1 oz / 30g. (yes)
Basic recipe for a vegetable soup (nutritious) 2 table spoons / 45g. (yes)
Lemon peel 1 teaspoon / 3g. (yes)
Lemon 1 teaspoon / 3g. (yes)
Oregano dried 2 teaspoons / 15g. (yes)
Ground 1 pinch / 1g. (yes)
Salt 1 pinch / 1g. (little)
Pepper (ground) 1 pinch / 1g. (yes)
Noodles (wheat, spaghetti) with egg 5/8 oz / 200g. (yes)
Salt 1 pinch / 1g. (little)
Olive oil 1 table spoon / 15g. (yes)

Onion (spring onion) 2 pieces / 40g. (yes)
Zucchini 5/8 lbs - 8oz / 250g. (recommended)

Cooking instructions:
Mix Basil, olive oil, grated almonds, parmesan, vegetable broth and grated lemon peel to a smooth cream puree.
Season the pesto with salt, oregano, cumin and pepper.

Boil the spaghetti with a little salt in plenty of water.

Heat the olive oil in a pan and fry the spring onions while stirring. Add zucchini and fry briefly with stirring. The zucchini should be soft with a bite. Season the zucchini with salt.

In a bowl, mix well-drained spaghetti with zucchini and pesto. Season the spaghetti with salt and pepper.

Recommended for dysphagia, loss of appetite, potassium and magnesium requirements.

10 Effects of food

10.1 Use ingredients: recommendable

Acai powder
Apple (sour)
Apple (sweet)
Apple puree
Asparagus (green or white)
Beans (green, fresh)
Bitter Herb liqueur
Blackberry´s
Borage
Broccoli
Brussels sprouts
Carrot
Carrot (Early Carrot)
Carrot juice without sugar
Cauliflower
Celery root
Celery sticks
Cherry
Cherry (sour)
Chicory
Chinese cabbage
Cod
Corn germ oil
Cranberry
Cranberry juice
Cream 10% coffee cream
Cucumber
Cucumber (bitter)
Cucumber (spicy cucumber)
Curd cheese 20%
Currant (black)
Currant (red)
Currant (white)
Fennel
Fish pieces mixed (fresh water)
Fox nut, gorgon nut, makhana
Gourd
Herbal tea mix
Herring
Hibiscus
Juniper berry
Kohlrabi
Kudzu
Lamb's lettuce
Lamb's lettuce
Leaf salads (bitter)
Lentils
Lettuce
Lily bulbs

Linseed oil
Mackerel
Manioc flour
Mascarpone cheese
Mediterranean fish (cod, plaice,
haddock, sea eel, mackerel)
Muesli
Noodles (whole grain) with egg
Oat flakes (whole grain)
Oat fusion (baby food)
Peaches
Peaches (canned)
Pear
Peppers
Plaice
Plum
Plums
Processed cheese 12%
Radicchio
Radish
Radish (white, green, purple-red)
Radish horseradish
Rapeseed oil
Raspberry
Red beet
Red cabbage
Rhubarb
Rice (whole grain)
Rice mash
Rice wild (nature rice)
Rose hip
Rose hip tea
Rosefish
Rucola
Rye wholemeal bread
Salmon
Savory
Savoy cabbage / kale
Sesame oil
Soya Cuisine (soy cream)
Soybeans
Strawberries
Tomato
Trout
Tuna
Turkey breast meat
Turnip
Turnips
Vegetable juice

Walnuts
Watermelon
Wax gourd
Wheat bran
Wheat flour whole grain
Wheat germ oil
Wheat/Rye/Gray-black bread with yeast

White cabbage
Whole grain bread
Wholemeal flour
Wild herbs
Yogurt (natural, 1.5% fat)
Zucchini

10.2 Use ingredients: yes

Acerola fruit nectar or powder
Adzuki beans
Agar agar (kelp)
Agave nectar
Agrimony
Almond
Almond marzipan
Almond milk
Almond puree
Aloe juice
Amaranth
Amaranth Pops
Anchovy / Sardine
Angelica root
Anise (Common Fennel)
Apple juice (natural cloudy)
Apricot
Apricot dried
Apricot jam
Apricot nectar
Apricots
Apricots juice
Arrowroot
Artichoke
Aubergine
Avocado
Baking powder
Balm
Bamboo shoots
Banana
Banana (cooking banana)
Banchatee (green tea)
barberry
Barley
Barley flour
Barley grass powder
Barley grouts
Barley malt
Barley not peeled
Basic recipe for a beef soup
Basic recipe for a beef soup (warming)
Basic recipe for a chicken soup
(warming)
Basic recipe for a duck soup

Basic recipe for a fish soup
Basic recipe for a rice soup (Congee)
Basic recipe for a vegetable soup
(nutritious)
Basil
Basil (fresh)
Batavia
Bay leaf
Bean oil
Bearberry leaf
Beef bone marrow
Beef fillet
Beef heart
Beef heart (calf)
Beef lungs (calf)
Beef meat
Beef meat (calf)
Beef meatbones
Beef Oxtail pieces
Beef soup meat
Beef stomach
Berries of the season
Berry juice
Bitter Lemon
Bitter orange peel
Black beans
Black caraway
Black fungus mushroom
Black tea
Blackberry dried (unripe fruit)
Blackberry jam
Blackberry leaves
Black-eyed peas
Blackthorn (Sloe)
Blue mallow tee
Blueberry
Blueberry dried
Blueberry jam
Blueberry juice
Bocksdorn fruits (Fructus Lycii, Goji,
goji berry dried
Boletus mushroom
Borage oil
Boxhorn clover seeds

Brazil nuts
Bread with carob kernel flour
Breadcrumbs (wheat bread, bread roll)
Brie cheese
Broad beans (thick beans)
Buckbean
Buckwheat
Buckwheat (roasted) Kasha
Buckwheat whole grain
Bulgur (cereals)
Burdock root tea
Bush beans
Butter (half fat)
Butter beans white
Butter organic
Buttermilk
Calamari
Camembert
Cantaloupe
Capers in olive oil
Carambola (Star fruit)
Cardamom
Carob flour, St. john's bread
Carp
Cashews
Caviar
Cereal coffee
Chamomile
Chamomile tea
Champignon
Channa-Dal
Chanterelle
Chard
Chenpi (chinese tangerine bowl)
Cherry compote
Cherry juice
Chervil
Chervil dried
Chestnut puree
Chestnuts
Chicken Blood
Chicken egg
Chicken egg white
Chicken heart
Chicken meat
Chicken stomach
Chickpeas
Chickweed
Chili (pod or ground)
Chinese pearl barley
Chives
Chlorella (fresh water)
Chrysanthemum blossom tea
Cinnamon ground

Cinnamon sticks
Clementine
Clementines
Clove
Cocoa
Coconut flakes
Coconut grated
Coconut meat
Coconut milk
Codfish
Coffee
Coix (seeds) YiYi Ren
Cola drink (low calorie)
Compote (fruits of the season)
Cooking oil
Coriander
Coriander (fresh)
Corn
Corn (fast polenta)
Corn (roasted)
Corn flour
Corn Grease (Polenta)
Corn silk tea
Corn starch
Cottage cheese
Couscous
Cow's milk (1.5% fat)
Cow's milk (whole milk 3.5% fat)
Crab
Cranberries
Cranberry
Cranberry jam
Cream sour 10%
Cream sour 20%
Cream sour 30%
Creamer
Créme fraiche cheese
Cress
Crispbread
Crucian
Cumin (Caraway seed)
Curcuma
Curd cheese 40%
Currant jam (black)
Currant jam (red)
Currant juice (black)
Currants (black)
Currants (red)
Curry
Curry paste red
Daisy
Dandelion (young plants)
Dandelion juice
Dandelionroots tea

Dashi
Dates dried
Dates red
Deer meat
Deer meat
Deer's Bones
Deer's kidneys
Dill
Duck (heart)
Duck (slaughtered)
Ducks egg
Dulse (seaweed)
Dyer's broom herb
Edam cheese
Eel
Eel smoked
Elderberries
Elderberry blossom tee
Emmental cheese
Endive salad
Evening primrose oil
Fennel seeds ground
Fennel tea
Fenugreek (Trigonella foenum-graecum)
Feta cheese
Feta cheese
Fig
Fig dried
Fish sauce
Flounder
Flower pollen
French beans
Fresh cheese
Fresh cheese from soya
Fresh cheese with herbs
Freshwater crab
Freshwater fish
Fructose (glucose)
Fruit mix juice
Fruit tea
Gail plum
Galangal
Garam Masala powder
Garlic
Gelatin white
Gelee Royal
Gentian root
Gentian root tea
Ginger fresh
Ginger oil
Ginger powder
Ginkgo fruit
Ginseng

Ginseng root
Goat
Goat and sheep's blood
Goat and sheep's brain
Goat and sheep's milk
Goat and sheep's stomach
Goat cheese
Goose
Goose blood
Goose egg
Goose fat
Goose parts
Gooseberry
Gorgonzola
Gouda cheese
Grape juice red
Grape juice white
Grapefruit (Pomelo)
Grapefruit dried peel
Grapefruit juice
Grapes red
Grapes white
Grapeseed oil
Grass carp
Green spelt
Green tea
Greengage
Ground
Ground caraway
Guava
Halibut (Flatfish)
Hawthorn
Hazelnuts
Herbs bitter
Herbs of Provence
Herbs various
Herbs wild
Hibiscus tea
Hijiki
Hokkaido pumpkin
Honey
Hop
Horehound leaves
Horse meat
Hyssop
Iceberg lettuce
Jasmine blossoms tee
Jellyfish
Kaki plum
Kalmus
Kefir
Kidney beans (red)
King Solomon's-seal
Kiwi

Kombu seaweed (Saccharina japonica)
Kukicha tea
Kumquats
Ladyfingers
Lamb bones
Lamb meat
Lamb shoulder
Lavender blossoms
Leek
Lemon
Lemon Balm (dried)
Lemon Balm (fresh)
Lemon juice
Lemon peel
Lemongrass
Lentils black
Lentils red
Lentils yellow
Licorice root tea
Lima beans
Lime
Lime blossom tea
Linseed
Linseed (crushed)
Liver smoothing tea
Lobster
Longane
Loquate / Japanese medlar
Lotus roots
Lotus seeds
Lovage
Lovage seeds
Luo Han Guo fruit
Lychee
Lychee in Preserved
Lye roll
Mallow (Malva sylvestris) blossom tea
Malt
Mango
Mango juice
Maple syrup
Mare's milk
Margarine
Margarine (diet)
Marjoram
Medlar
Millet
Millet flakes
Mineral water
Mirabelle plum
Miso
Miso black (fermented)
Miso paste (soy bean paste)
Mixed Pickles

Mold cheese
Morel (black, dried)
Morel, dried
Mozzarella
Mu Erh Mushroom
Mulberry fruit
Mulled Wine Spice
Mullet
Multi-grain bread (gray bread)
Mung bean
Mung bean sprouting
Mussels
Mustard
Mustard Dijon
Mustard medium hot
Mustard seeds
Mustard sweet
Mutton
Mutton
Nasturtium (nose-twister or nose-tweaker)
Nectarine
Nettles
Noodles (wheat) with egg
Noodles (wheat, lasagne) with egg
Noodles (wheat, ribbon noodles) with egg
Noodles (wheat, spaghetti) with egg
Nori, purple seaweed, red algae
Nutmeg
Oat
Oat flakes roasted
Oat flour
Oat meal
Oat milk
Octopus
Octopus
Okra
Olive oil
Olives
Olives green
Onion (shallot)
Onion (spring onion)
Onion read
Onion white
Orange
Orange blossom
Orange dried peel
Orange grated peel
Orange jam
Orange juice
Orange peel
Oregano dried
Oregano fresh

Oyster mushroom
Oyster shell powder
Oysters
Palm oil
Papaya
Parmesan
Parsley
Parsley root
Parsnip
Passion blossoms tea
Passion fruit
Peanut butter
Peanut oil
Peanuts
Pear juice
Pearl barley
Pearl barley
Peas
Peas, green
Pepper (ground)
Pepper Cayenne
Pepper powder (hot)
Pepper white (ground)
Peppercorns
Peppermint
Peppermint tea
Pepperoni
Pepperoni, red, pitted, halved
Pepperoni, yellow, pitted, halved
Peppers (rose peppers)
Peppers (sweet)
Peppers powder
Perch
Pheasant
Pickle
Pig blood
Pigeon
Pigeon egg
Pimento
Pine nuts
Pineapple
Pineapple (from a can)
Pineapple juice without sugar
Pinto beans speckled
Pistachios
Plum dried
Pomegranate
Poppy
Pork Bacon
Pork brain
Pork fat (lard)
Pork ham
Pork ham cooked
Pork ham smoked

Pork knuckle
Pork lung
Pork marrow bones
Pork meat
Pork sausage (Bratwurst)
Pork skin
Pork stomach
Pork/beef sausage (smoked)
Pork's intestine
Potato
Potato (mealy)
Potato flour
Prickly pear
processed cheese 30%
Psyllium seed
Pudding powder vanilla
Puff pastry
Pumpernickel (dark bread)
Pumpkin
Pumpkin seed oil
Pumpkin seeds
Quail
Quail egg
Quince
Quinoa
Rabbit
Rabbit (wild)
Rabbit liver
Rabbit meat
Radish black
Radish leaves
Raisins
Raspberry dried (immature)
Raspberry jam
Raspberry leaf tea
Red berry (without sugar)
Reishi mushroom
Ribworttea
Rice (fragrance)
Rice (Gaoliang / Sorghum)
Rice Basmati
Rice black
Rice flour
Rice long grain rice
Rice malt
Rice noodles
Rice red
Rice round grain
Rice starch
Rice sticky
Rice sweet
Rice variety any
Romaine lettuce / lettuce salad
Rose blossom tea

Rose leaf tea
Rosemary
Rusk
Rye
Rye flour
Safflower (Dyer's thistle / Hong Hua)
Saffron
Sage
Sago (cereals)
Sake
Salsify
Salt (herbal)
Sauerkraut (cutted cabbage fermented)
Sea buckthorn
Sea cucumber
Seacrab
Sesame oil roasted
Sesame paste (Tahini)
Sesame, black
Sesame, white
Shark
Sheep's milk
Sheep's milk yoghurt
Shiitake, dried
Shrimp
Shrimps
Skim milk powder
Slug
Sorrel
Sour cherries
Sour cream 15% fat
Sour milk
Sour milk cheese 20%
Sourdough
Soy flour
Soy noodles
Soy sauce
Soy Tofu
Soy Tofu smoked
Soybean milk
Soybean oil
Soybeans, black
Soybeans, blacks, fermented
Soybeans, yellow
Spelled (Dark) bread
Spelled flakes
Spelled grain
Spelled semolina
Spelled wholemeal flour
Spinach
Spiny lobsters
Spurdog (spiny dogfish, Schillerlocken)
St. Benedict's thistle, blessed thistle, holy thistle, spotted thistle

Star anise
Stevia (candyleaf, sweetleaf)
Strawberry jam
Strawberry Juice
Sugar fructose - fruit sugar
Sugar glucose - grapes sugar
Sugar Milk Sugar
Sugar substitute (sweetener)
Sunflower oil
Sunflower seeds
Sweet potato
Tabasco
Tangerine
Tarragon (Estragon)
Tea mixture uric acid lowering
Thistle oil
Thyme
Thyme dried
Toast bread (whole grain)
Tomato dried
Tomato juice
Tomato paste
Tomato puree
Tonic Water
Topinambur
Trout (smoked)
Truffle
Tsampa (roasted barley flour)
Turkey ham
Turmeric (yellow root)
Umeboshi paste
Umeboshi plums (Japanese apricots)
Valerian
Vanilla
Vanilla pod
Vanilla powder
Vanilla sugar natural
Vinegar (Apple vinegar)
Vinegar (Red wine vinegar)
Vinegar Aceto Balsamico
Vinegar Aceto Balsamico white
Wakame
Walnut oil
Walnuts roasted
Water
Water hot
Wheat
Wheat bulgur
Wheat flakes
Wheat flatbread/pita bread
Wheat flour
Wheat semolina
Wheat semolina for children
Wheatgrass juice

Wheatgrass powder
Whey
White beans
Whitefish
Wild boar meat
Wild garlic (garlic spinach)
Wild strawberries
Wormwood herb

Yam root, yam root tuber
Yarrow
Yarrow tea
Yeast
Yew nut
Yoghurt vanilla
Yogi tea
Yogurt (natural, 3.5% fat)

10.3 Use ingredients: little

Beef kidney
Beef liver
Beer (alcohol-free)
Beer (alcohol-reduced)
Beer (Pils)
Beer (Top-fermented German dark beer)
Bitter liqueur
Bread roll
Brown ale
Campari
Chicken liver
Chicken yolk
Chocolate
Chocolate (Diabetic)
Clarified butter
Coconut fat
Cola drink
Cream (30% fat)
Cream, sweet 30%
Fernet Branca (herbal bitter liqueur)
Fish innards
Fish remains
Ginseng liqueur
Goat and sheep's liver
Honey wine (Met)
Lamb kidneys
Lamb liver
Lychee liqueur
Martini

Mayonnaise 50%
Mayonnaise 80%
Peanut (roasted)
Pork heart
Pork kidneys
Pork Lard
Pork liver
Prosecco
Red wine
Rum
Salt
Sherry (whine)
Spirit
Sugar - icing sugar
Sugar brown
Sugar candy white
Sugar cane sugar
Sugar molasses
Sugar palm sugar
Sugar white
Wheat beer
White bread (baguette)
White bread (pretzel sticks)
White bread (roll)
White bread (wheat bread)
White breadcrumbs
White dumpling bread (wheat bread cut into chunks)
White wine
Wormwood

10.4 Do not use contra-acting foods

Supplementary nutrition

11 Herbs and their effects

11.1 Basil

It has a beneficial effect on flatulence and nausea, relaxing and soothing. Good to fight emphysema, bronchitis, whooping cough, high blood pressure, headache, mouth odor, warts, hiccup, gout, migraine.

11.2 Mugwort

Reduces bleeding, alleviates pain. In the kitchen, mugwort is used as a spice for fat food. Since it contains many bitter substances, it boosts fat burning and promotes digestion.

11.3 Savory

Stomach-strengthening, soothing and appetizing. Ideal for prevent colds, strengthens the immune system. In case of incontinence or nocturnal wetting (not for children), put the beans in liquor for libido.

11.4 Nettles

Promotes urination. Tea or juice, cleanses the blood and the kidneys, supports prostate problems, inhibit the formation of inflammation, pain-relieving.

11.5 Dill

The medicinal and spice herb has an antispasmodic effect and stimulates gastric juice production. Good to fight flatulence. Antispasmodic for gastrointestinal discomfort.

11.6 Chamomile

Antispasmodic and anti-inflammatory for digestive disorders, soothes the nerves and promotes good sleep. Applied externally, it heals wounds in the mouth-throat area and the skin. Strengthens eyesight.

11.7 Chervil dried

Forces urination, detoxifying, blood-purifying and blood-pressure-reducing effects.

11.8 Coriander

The essential oils are appetizing, digestive, cramping and soothing in stomach and intestinal disorders.

11.9 Herbs various

Appetizing, lots of trace elements and vitamins

11.10 Cress

Diuretic, supports urination. Good to fight dry mouth, inner agitation, sore throat, diabetes, kidney stones, gastrointestinal complaints, lung problems, menstrual cramps or cancer.

11.11 Chives

Bactericide, prevents cancer, strengthens gastric juice production, promotes digestion and blood circulation, promotes growth, triggers stagnation.

11.12 Lovage

Stimulates digestion, reduces pain. Extracts of the root are used to flush out urinary tract infections and prevent kidney gravel.

11.13 Lily bulbs

Calms nerves, good to fight scaly skin. The onions and the petals are added to ointments in the Orient, which can heal muscles and tendons. White lily (astringent).

11.14 Dandelion (young plants)

Detoxifies, relieves inflammation. Regulates digestion, helps with rheumatism, releases kidney stones, leaves pimples and chronic skin disorders disappear.

11.15 Marjoram

Helps to digest fat foods, strengthens digestive organs, helps to fight colds, strengthens menstruation, promotes skin healing.

11.16   Oregano fresh

It has an anti-digestive, calming and nerve-strengthening effect, helps to fight cramping stomach and intestinal disorders. The ingredient Carvacrol has an anti-inflammatory effect.

11.17   Parsley

Stimulates liver function, detoxifies. Forces urinating. Relieves flatulence. Digestive and menstrual stimulating, birth-accelerating, memory-enhancing, blood-purifying, skin-smoothing.

11.18   Peppermint

Relaxes, frees the lungs and the nose (inhale), regulates the cycle. Stimulates bile flow and bile production, antispasmodic in gastrointestinal disorders, antimicrobial and antiviral.

11.19   Rosemary

Promotes digestion, relieves bloating, strengthens lung, spleen and kidney. Affects the circulation and nerves. Appetizing. Baths help to fight circulatory disorders as well as with gout and rheumatism.

11.20   Sage

Good to fight yeast infections. The leaves have a digestive effect and are used in greasy foods. Antiperspirant effect. Helps to relieve coughing attacks. Dries out (TCM).

11.21   Sorrel

Astringent, hematopoietic, purifies the blood, diuretic. Good to fight liver weakness, upset stomach, indigestion, constipation, diarrhea, worms, scurvy, anemia, women's complaints, wounds, skin rashes, boils, ulcers, swelling.

11.22   Black caraway

Detoxifying, immunoregulatory. In addition, the oil should stimulate the formation of bone marrow cells and generally protect body cells from viruses.

11.23 Thyme dried

Disinfecting. It stimulates the blood circulation, increases the appetite and helps to digest fat meat better. Strengthens lungs and spleen (TCM).

11.24 King Solomon's-seal

Used to repair wounds or damaged tissue. Good to fight dry cough, earlier also tuberculosis and dysentery, as well as diarrhea and hemorrhoids.

11.25 Yam root, yam root tuber

Solves cramps (in the gastrointestinal tract). Digestive through increased bile production. Anti-inflammatory in rheumatic diseases. Mucolytic agent for coughing. Relief of menopausal symptoms.

11.26 Lemongrass

Reduction of flatulence, antimicrobial, appetizing. Prevention of influenza. Good to fight infections in the mouth and throat.

11.27 Lemon Balm (fresh)

Stimulating, antibacterial, encouraging, relaxing, antispasmodic, cooling, antipyretic, analgesic, sweat-inducing, virus-inhibiting. Good for colds, fever, flu, cough, bronchitis, asthma, loss of appetite, bloating, heartburn.

12 Basics of Nutrition

The basic principles of nutrition described herein are general recommendations. They are not aimed at a specific form of therapy. Recommendations concerning a therapy have priority.

12.1 Nutrition

Regular meals in a relaxed atmosphere. A warm breakfast is considered a good start into the day.
The main meals ought to be taken for lunch – supper in the early evening. Pay attention to feeling hungry or sated: don't eat too much nor remain hungry is the rule
Prepare the meals freshly from natural, regional products. Frozen, heat-conserved, industrially prepared or foodstuffs cooked in the microwave oven are rejected.
Choice of foodstuffs according to the season: more cooling food in summer, more warming food in winter.
Eat cooked food at least twice a day. Food and drinks ought to be lukewarm, never ice-cold or hot.
Raw vegetables, briefly cooked vegetables, freshly squeezed juices and mineral water are not recommended. Milk and dairy products are only included in the diet if they don't cause problems.
Don't use therapeutic recipes over a longer period without consulting your doctor or therapist.

Varied food
Enjoy the diversity of foodstuffs. Characteristics of a balanced nutrition are variety, suitable combination and a balanced quantity of rich and low energy foodstuffs (on one hand avoiding undersupply with essential nutrients and on the other hand to take to many undesirable substances).

A lot of Cereal Products - and Potatoes
Bread, pasta, rice, cereal flakes (best wholemeal) as well as potatoes contain almost no fat, but many vitamins, mineral nutrients, trace elements, roughage and secondary plant substances. These foodstuffs ought to be taken with low-fat side dishes.

Vegetables and Fruit – „Take Five" every day ...
5 portions of vegetables and fruit a day, as fresh as possible, briefly cooked, or maybe one portion as a juice – ideal as a side dish to every meal as well as snack between meals: Thus a lot of vitamins, mineral nutrients as well as roughage and secondary plant substances

Daily milk and dairy products
Milk and Dairy Products every Day, once or twice per Week Fish; meat, sausages as well as eggs moderately. These foodstuffs contain valuable nutrients like calcium in the milk, iodine selenium and omega-3 fat acids in saltwater fish. Meat is favorable due to its high content of disposable iron and the vitamins B1, B6 and B12. Quantities of 300 – 600 g meat and sausage per week are sufficient. Prefer low-fat products, especially in meat- and dairy products.

Low-fat and fatty Foodstuffs
Fat supplies us with essential fat acids and fatty foodstuffs contain also fat-soluble vitamins. Fat is high in energy; therefore much fat in the food may cause overweight, possibly also cancer. Too many saturated fat acids may further a tendency for cardio-vascular diseases in the long term. Prefer vegetable oils and fats (e.g. rapeseed-, olive-, soya-oils and solid fats produced therefrom). Beware of invisible fat in meat- and dairy products, pastry and sweets as well as in fast-food and convenience foods. 70 – 90 g fat per day is sufficient.

Moderately Sugar and Salt
Take sugar and foods/drinks containing various kinds of sugar (e.g. glucose syrup) only occasionally. Use herbs and spices as well as a little salt creatively. Prefer salt containing iodine.

Plenty of Liquids
Water is absolutely essential. Drink 1-2 l liquids every day. Prefer water (with or without gas) and other low-calorie drinks. Alcoholic drinks should not be taken.

Tasty Dishes, carefully cooked
Cook the meals with as low temperatures and as short as possible, using little water and fat – this preserves the original taste, keeps the nutrients intact and prevents the production of harmful compounds.

Take time and enjoy the food
Take your Time and enjoy your Food
Eating consciously helps to eat right. The eye enjoys food, too. It's fun, invites to enjoy varied dishes and stimulates the feeling of satiety.

Watch your Weight and stay in Motion
A balanced diet and a lot of exercise and sport (30 – 60 min/day) are a healthy combination. The right weight furthers well-being and health. Thermals, directional effectiveness, digestive power

There are various criteria for judging the effectiveness of herbs and foodstuffs.

The use of certain herbs and ingredients is based on observations of the effects on the body which these foodstuffs, herbs and spices show after having eaten them. The medical science has developed following system: Every ingredient or herb has a directional effectiveness. Furthermore, there are herbs which have a special effect on certain organs.

The basic condition for a healthy metabolism is to obtain sufficient energy from food and that the digestive process doesn't use too much energy. An easily digestible meal makes content and sated, doesn't cause flatulence and fatigue after the meal. The perfect spices increase the healthiness of our meals. Very often, just small doses of herbs and spices will suffice. They are not used to make us sated, but to help our digestive organs to digest the food.

12.2 Recipes

The recipes list the ingredients to be used and the cooking instructions show how the dish is prepared. The list of ingredients shows the concerned quantities as well as the relevance for the therapy. If you find „less than mentioned", try to comply or find an alternative from the „list of recommended foodstuffs". Mostly it shall result just in a small change of taste when you simply avoid this ingredient.

Mild cooking methods: boiling, stewing, poaching, steaming
Strong cooking methods: barbecuing, roasting, frying, smoking
Balanced cooking methods: deep-frying, baking brick
Deep-freezing and warming in the microwave oven should be avoided (denaturalization).

12.3 Foodstuffs

Foodstuffs have an effect on body and soul like medicinal herbs, only a very much milder one. Dietary advice is mainly based on regional foodstuffs. The knowledge about the effects of each foodstuff and the knowledge, when which foodstuff shall be used, is based on the orthodoschool of medicine. Use ecologic-organic products, if possible. As everything should be cooked for a long time due to a better digestability and very rarely eaten raw, the food agrees with everyone.

The classification of the foodstuffs according to their effect on the body is the basis in order to achieve a harmonious status of health.

Dietary advisors do not recommend certain foodstuffs for everyone. The individual diet is tailor-made for the individual constitution.

Buy only fresh and ripe fruit and vegetables. You ought to leave unripe fruit and vegetables and such with brown spots and wilted leaves behind in the market. In this case take deep-frozen goods (never ready-to-serve dishes!). Fruit and vegetables are deep-frozen immediately after harvesting and often contain more vitamins and minerals than the goods from the vegetable shelf. Whereas conserved or tinned goods contain very much less biological substances. Also, salt, sugar and others are mostly added to the latter. Never leave the foodstuffs in the water after washing them to avoid that many vital substances get drowned. Clean salads, fruit and vegetables immediately before serving.

Please make sure of the hygienic processing of foodstuffs. Clean your salads, fruit and vegetables carefully. When cooking with meat, prepare all ingredients first and then process the meat products. Clean the worktop and tools very carefully. Wooden surfaces ought to be treated with a mild disinfectant regularly in order to reduce germination.

Store fruit and vegetables separately, if possible. Harvested fruit and vegetables are still alive and emit e.g. ethylene gas, which makes other products ripen and age faster. Keep meat and fish in the closed packaging or store them in the fridge in closed containers.

12.4 Herbs

There are some basic rules for storing medicinal herbs. On principle, herbs must be protected from direct sunlight, humidity and heat.

Containers for the storage of herbs may be glasses, ceramic jars and even plastic containers. However, plastic is a rather unsuitable material and should only be a short-term solution. In case of glass containers, use a dark material.

Medicinal herbs cannot be kept for any long period. The shelf life of herbs is limited. However, it can be prolonged with suitable storage. The place should be dark, rather cool and absolutely dry. A wooden medicine cabinet, placed not directly next to a source of heat, would be ideal. Never buy large quantities of herbs so as not to have to throw them away. Label the container with the name of the herb and the date of harvesting or processing.

13 Other dietic-books

The following syndromes of dietetics, TCM or for a therapy supplement for cancer are available.

Dietetics

E001. Nutrition of the infant - baby food
E002. Nutrition during lactation
E003. Nutrition in old age
E004. Nutrition of children and adolescents
E005. Nutrition of athletes
E006. Light weight
E007. Pregnancy
E008. Full food

Protein and electrolyte - kidneys
E009. (hemodialysis) dialysis treatment
E010. Acute renal failure
E011. Chronic renal insufficiency
E012. Nephrotic syndrome
E013. Kidney stones (nephrolithiasis)

Gastrointestinal tract - pancreas
E014. Acute pancreatitis (inflammation of the pancreas)
E015. Chronic pancreatitis (inflammation of the pancreas)

Gastrointestinal tract - small intestine and large intestine
E016. Acute obstipation (constipation)
E017. Chronic obstipation (constipation)
E018. Colon irritabile
E019. Diverticulitis
E020. Acquired lactose intolerance (lactose malabsorption)
E021. Fructose malabsorption
E022. Glutensensitive enteropathy (celiac disease)
E023. Colectomy
E024. Short Bowel Syndrome

Gastrointestinal tract - liver, gallbladder, bile ducts
E025. Acute and chronic hepatitis (inflammation of the liver)
E026. Cholelithiasis (bile stones)
E027. fatty liver
E028. cirrhosis

Gastrointestinal tract - Stomach and duodenal intestine
E029. Acute gastritis
E030. Chronic gastritis
E031. Stomach bleeding
E032. Ulcus ventriculi and duodenal ulcer
E033. Condition after gastric surgery

Gastrointestinal tract - oral cavity and esophagus
E034. Stomatitis
E035. Esophageal carcinoma (esophageal cancer)
E036. Refluosophagitis (heartburn)

Special diseases
E037. Phenylketonuria (PKU)
E038. Rheumatic joint diseases

Metabolism
E039. Obesity (overweight)
E040. Diabetes mellitus
E041. Eating disorders (underweight)

Fat metabolism
E042. Hypercholesterolaemia (increased cholesterol level)
E043. Hepatic Encephalopathy

Heart and circulation
E044. Arteriosclerosis (arterial calcification)
E045. Heart insufficiency
E046. Hypertension
E047. Hyperuricaemia and gout

Changed nutrient requirements
E048. In case of fever
E049. For malignant diseases
E050. After burns
E051. Radiation and chemotherapy

CANCER
E100. Pancreatic cancer
E101. Bladder cancer
E102. Blood cancer (leukemia)
E103. Breast cancer
E104. Colorectal cancer
E105. Gastric cancer
E106. Kidney cancer
E107. Esophageal cancer

TCM
E200. Bladder - moisture heat in the bladder
E201. Bladder - moisture and cold in the bladder
E202. Bladder - emptiness and cold in the bladder
E203. Large intestine - external cold affects the large intestine
E204. Large intestine - moisture heat in the large intestine
E205. Large intestine - heat blocks the intestine II acute
E206. Large intestine - dryness of the colon
E207. Large intestine - Yang deficiency (cold)
E208. Heart - Blood insufficiency
E209. Heart - Blood stagnation
E210. Heart - Fire
E211. Heart - Hot mucus clogs the heart pores

E212. Heart - Cold mucus clogs the heart pores
E213. Heart - Qi deficiency
E214. Heart - Yang deficiency
E215. Heart - Yin deficiency
E216. Liver - Ascending Liver Yang
E217. Liver - Blood deficiency
E218. Liver - Blood stagnation
E219. Liver - Moisture heat in liver and gall bladder
E220. Liver - Fire
E221. Liver - Gall bladder Qi-Empty
E222. Liver - Cold in the liver meridian
E223. Liver - Qi stagnation
E224. Liver - Wind
E225. Liver - Wind with ascending liver Yang
E226. Liver - Wind with blood anemic
E227. Liver - Wind with extreme heat
E228. Lung - Qi deficiency
E229. Lung - Mucus-moisture in the lungs
E230. Lung - Mucus-heat in the lungs
E231. Lung - Mucus-cold in the lungs
E232. Lung - Dryness of the lungs
E233. Lung - Wind-heat attacks the lungs
E234. Lung - Wind-cold affects the lungs
E235. Lung - Yin deficiency
E236. Stomach - Bloodstagnation
E237. Stomach - Fire
E238. Stomach - Cold with liquid
E239. Stomach - Nutrition stagnation
E240. Stomach - Qi deficiency
E241. Stomach - Rebellious Qi
E242. Stomach - Yin Emptiness
E243. Spleen - Heat and moisture attack the spleen
E244. Spleen - Coldness and moisture affects the spleen
E245. Spleen - Qi deficiency
E246. Spleen - Qi deficiency + Declining spleen Qi
E247. Spleen - Qi deficiency + spleen does not control the blood
E248. Spleen - Yang deficiency
E249. Kidney - Heart and kidney no longer communicate
E250. Kidney - Jing deficiency
E251. Kidney - Kidneys cannot receive the Qi
E252. Kidney - Qi is not stable
E253. Kidney - Yang deficiency
E254. Kidney - Yin deficiency

For further information visit di-book.com.